HOW TO GET FOLLOWERS ON

twitter

HOW TO GET FOLLOWERS ON twitter

100 ways to find and keep followers who want to hear what you have to say.

Steve Burns

Also by Steve Burns
How I Made Money Using the Nicolas Darvas System
New Trader, Rich Trader

Contents

Foreword

As the owner and founder of AroundTheOctagon.com I pride myself on being 'tech-savy'. I taught myself Wordpress and developed one of the top MMA websites in the world in a few months.

Networking was key in the growth of ATO (aroundtheoctagon.com) and I was the king of Myspace until Facebook came along. It took a few days but Mark Zuckerberg didn't make his site that complicated and I was off an running adding friends and figuring out this new social networking empire.

Then Twitter came along. I'm going to be brutally honest here. I thought Twitter was the dumbest thing I had ever heard of. Who cares what you are doing? And if you only get 140 characters to write it, why even bother? The world had Facebook and as far as I was concerned Twitter was obsolete.

Later that year I kept hearing the words, tweet, trending, followers, and hash tags. I didn't know what it was but slowly I came around and decided to open a Twitter account. I was still a little skeptical but after spending a little time with it I decided that maybe Twitter could be useful after-all.

Every afternoon I would sit down and post stories from ATO into my Twitter and wait for the hits to come rolling in. I recall one afternoon I was going through the stats from the site and I noticed I had one or two hits coming from Twitter. I had a respectable following but it wasn't translating into hits for my site.

I thought that if I did a story about a UFC fighter I could put a "@" in front of his name and his followers could see and it click to my story but apparently it didn't work that way.

One day I was talking to Stephen about the stock market

and he told me that he had made some good investments recently and tweeted out advice to his followers. He had built his followers up to several thousand in a very short amount of time and I was intrigued about how he had done it. I explained to him that I had tried to use Twitter but I couldn't get my followers up and my tweets were going unread.

Stephen invited me into his office and showed me several useful tips on how to increase followers and how to properly use hash tags. I was dumbfounded at how simple it was. I left his office and raced to my laptop and applied the few tricks he showed me and within a few hours I was getting several hundred hits to ATO from my tweets. I wish I had gone to him sooner.

Twitter is here to stay and Stephen will show you in this book the ins and outs of the site. Pretty soon you too will have more followers and have your tweets reach a broader audience.

Allen Sircy
Founder and owner of AroundtheOctagon.com

Introduction

While other books will tell you all about how to use twitter, how to set up a profile, and inform you of the overwhelming amount of applications available to use with your twitter account. **This twitter book is only about one thing, how to get and keep followers.** The purpose of this book is to give twitter users who are frustrated with their small followings 100 ideas to help them build their following. By using the ideas found in this book consistently over a period of time it is possible to acquire 1000 followers. If you follow the principles of this book, you will see your followers grow. These are not my theories or opinions; these are the actual ideas I used to build my own twitter following to over 5000 in less than one year. Twitter has been a great help to me in both connecting with likeminded people and collaborating on business projects. Twitter was also the main outlet for promotions for my two published books that both reached the top 5% of all books sold on Amazon. I have helped others by sharing these ideas and I believe it will work for the readers of this book if they are patient and work on using these suggestions while also building a high quality twitter account through quality tweets.

Use the ideas that fit your twitter goals and personality and skip the ones you do not like. I believe everyone will find enough tips in this book to gain a substantial following of people who want to hear what you have to say.

PART I
Your Profile Page

1. Your Username

You are about to enter the twitterverse. What will be your name in this land of tweets, retweets, lists, quotes, links, and clever 140 character posts?

Creating your account name will be one of the most important things you decide when creating your account. In the twitterverse your name starts with the @ symbol. I will not insult the reader's intelligence by giving you a step by step on how to set up your account. I will assume that you can do this on the site, it is very user friendly.

What I will suggest is to find a user name that captures your main interests. Your name will be separate from your twitter @username. I am Steve Burns @SJosephBurns on twitter. @SteveBurns was taken so I used my first initial and middle name. I did not maximize my ability to get followers with my username; it should have reflected my interests. (Unfortunately I didn't have this book.) When I started my account I made the mistake of doing what we do on e-mail and trying to get my name as an address instead of my interests. There is no need to do this because your name is separate from your address. On twitter people will see your name next to your @username when they view your tweets.

They will see:
Your name @username

It will be a waste to have:
Your name @yourname

You want to have:
Your Name @yourmaininterest

My interests are stock and option trading. I am an author, book reviewer, and I love inspirational quotes along with social networking.

I should have tried a user name that would have captured attention in searches like:

@thestocktrader
@optiontrader2011
@traderandauthor
@traderontwitter

Of course all the most popular usernames have been taken so it will take several times to find an available one for you. But keep trying, you will find one. Just try to make minor changes to get as close as you can to the one you want.

Your username can lead followers to stumble upon you without you even looking for them. Twitter users look for people with popular theme names to follow. When people search "@stocktrader" on twitter under profile then all user-names similar show up. In this search I got:

@stocktrading2go
@STOCKTRADE_INFO
@Stocktrader69

This could lead people to follow you based on your @user-name. If you get a really popular username then this could bring you an additional fifty to one hundred followers or more who are interested in your subject.

The important thing is to make it match you, your core interests. It does no good to get people to follow you based on your username being @stocktrading2go and you only tweet about your personal life and not stock trading. Whatever you choose as your username, make sure your content matches it the majority of the time.

I wish I would have known this when I set up my account. But I have lived up to my username; my twitter is all about me and my interests.

2. You need a picture!

If you want people to follow you then let them see who they will be following. I know of many people on twitter who will not follow anyone who did not even go through the trouble of downloading a picture to their profile. The default egg is just not interesting or appealing. It gives the twitter account a bad image. This user didn't even go through the trouble to download a picture? How interesting can they be? How much effort will they even put in their tweets? They will move on and keep looking for more interesting users.

You do not have to download a picture of yourself. It can be an interesting image or picture that represents what you are all about. Something funny, something serious, or something that shows what you are interested in.

At one time I used a picture of a bookcase full of books. I also used the cover of my first book for a long time. I finally settled on a photo of myself, that represents me. Also to be more interesting I could at times put up a bear or a bull based on my stock market sentiment.

You could also do something similar based on your own personal interests. Like a NFL fan could post the helmet of his favorite team or the team he thought would win the super bowl during the season, and then change it as his opinion changed during the play offs. This would be one way to interest followers and have them curious to see your predictions and opinions. They may agree or argue with you. That is what you want though, interaction and followers. When you get interaction all their followers see you in their timeline and could join the conversation and become a follower if you share common beliefs, interests, or opinions.

Shy away from offensive pictures or images that are too

sexual or graphic in nature, you probably will not want the types of followers this attracts. Not to mention that twitter might shut down your account.

So replace the egg image with a picture that is worth a thousand words telling who you are or what you are interested in.

While the average profile picture may only get you a few followers and a really interesting one may by itself get you a few extra followers. No profile picture is pretty sure to make plenty of potential followers pass right by.

In my personal experience on twitter the egg profiles are the ones with the least action. Most of these were just set up and either never used or just set up to follow a few people.

So do not be an egg be a real person.

3. What are your interests?

Now you must put your interests on your profile. When real people decide to follow you they will use what you say under your picture and name to determine to follow you are not. If it is blank then you will likely be the recipient of spam followers only who do not care what you have to say and will likely not read any of your tweets ever.

Your interests should be placed under your profile settings in the spot labeled as "Bio". This is one of the most important things to get right to attract followers. I think it is important to put your interests here or who you are.

You could put:

I am a Stock trader, Option trader, Book reviewer, and Author of two books.

That might get people that were interested in those things to follow you, or people trying to sell you related things to follow you.

A better bio would be:

I am a Top 300 Amazon Book Reviewer: hear about the best books here first!

Or

I made $150,000 in the stock market, follow me and find out how you can too!

Or

Follow me to learn how to trade stocks and win!

You are really selling yourself in your bio. Express who you are and what you can give your followers. They like to feel informed and receive useful information.

Why should they follow you?

Why are you special?

What have you done that they can learn from?

What can you teach them?

You could have followers that look forward to when you write articles on your blog that is about a topic you are interested in. They follow you for the tweets that lead up to the post.

Some followers will follow stock traders for the hot stock tip or to learn how to trade. They may just want to understand how you trade.

You have to give your followers a reason to follow. You have to give them the impression on your bio that you will tweet out things that are interesting, informative, or clever. The follower needs to fill like they will learn something new or get entertained.

Use the generous 160 characters in your bio line to really show the potential followers who you are and what you have to give. The biggest decision to follow or not to follow will be made after reading your bio line on your profile, do not lose the opportunity, write to attract interest, sell what you have to offer potential followers.

4. The Link

Where are you trying to drive traffic? To your blog, website, facebook fan page, My Space profile, published book, or affiliate link? On your profile settings you get to post a link on your profile itself under web. Twitter itself recommends adding your homepage or blog on your profile.

Just be sure it is a destination that will inspire people to follow you. A link to a blog about a topic that the follower is interested in could inspire them to follow you on twitter and your blog. A link to an unrelated affiliate prescription drug page that pays per click will ensure that you are not followed and may even result in your account being reported for spam. If you are a top Amazon reviewer and your link is to your Amazon profile page that is also an affiliate link but will not offend anyone. It may work out perfect because you could have a link to your blog and email address on your Amazon page so a follower could connect with you off twitter in different ways.

Your link should really establish what you are about, and what information and content you have to share with followers. The link should not turn followers off it should be an extension to what you are tweeting about.

This link should inspire followers not disappoint them or turn them away. It should be interesting and engaging; it will represent what you are all about, don't miss this opportunity, and choose wisely.

5. Where are you?

Do not forget to enter your location. Twitter users are just beginning to use location to target who to follow. I have had a few follows from politicians in my state just seeking to get their name out there and hear what constituents have to say. Who knows, local politicians might actually use twitter for discussions and get the pulse of the voter. Entering your location will inspire a few local businesses and politicians to follow you which will get you closer to your 1000 goal with very little effort.

In the future when twitter monetizes the site and it grows in popularity location will be crucial information for target-ed advertising. One day, people may use twitter like facebook to find people they have not seen in ages. Why not go ahead and get your location in so people looking for you can find you and follow you.

6. Your tweet stream

If people see your twitter account and you have not tweeted since 2006, they will move on to someone else who is actually tweeting. While that is an exaggeration many accounts on twitter have been abandoned. Many have not had tweets since 2009. Any observant user will look at your tweet stream before following you. If you have not tweeted in a week they will likely assume you are not very active and move on to others who are.

People that are following accounts even though they have not tweeted in months are probably just randomly following any way and may just be planning to spam you. It is unlikely they really care enough to read tweets any way if they have not noticed your tweet activity.

It is important to tweet at least daily if you want to keep an engaged audience. Ideally you could tweet in the morning, afternoon, and evening to really catch your followers that are reading your tweets. Different people have a habit of reading their tweet stream at different times of day.

Potential followers will also likely see and read your last two or three tweets so end with some good material for the day. It could turn a potential follower away if your last tweet is too pushy or too dull. Always end with your best to set yourself up to look interesting for your potential followers that check out your profile between tweets.

Also if you have an affiliate account that you push on twitter ensure that these tie in naturally with your tweet stream. You should send out an affiliate link for Amazon when you actually review a product. Or recommend a book through a link when it fits in the context of a discussion. No real follower will follow a twitter user where their last five tweets were exactly the same thing, pushing a link to sell something. That sets off all the spammer alarm bells and the follower moves on.

Leave an attractive tweet stream to gain more followers. This is a very important step to move you toward your 1000 follower goal.

7. Communicate

Twitter is not just a site to broadcast and tell what's happening. It is also a modern form of communication. Just like texting is a brief condensed form of communication for phones, tweeting is a brief form of communication from a website that is many times read on phones. A tweet is not just a 140 character message you broadcast. If you are sending out truly great tweets, some thought provoking, some informative, and some that ask for opinions. Then you will receive replies to your tweets. Replies show up in the senders tweet stream. When you reply to someone else your reply shows up in your tweet stream. You can see the whole conversation at your home page under your @mentions tab.

You want to reply to tweets so potential followers will know:

1. That you read others tweets.
2. Interact with your followers.
3. You are on twitter to share and discuss not spam.
4. You have friends on twitter.
5. That if they follow you they could be part of a network on twitter.

Timelines that have replies look much more inviting than just a continuous unbroken broadcast. When you find a tweet interesting or have a question or thought to add, reply. You can also reply to tweets that mention you or any products or business that you are involved with promoting. Sending out a thank you reply on twitter goes a long way to build goodwill with followers.

You can send a direct tweet to someone by simply tweeting out @their username, if they have their cell phone set up to receive direct tweets then they will receive it on their phone through either a text of twitter phone app. Followers like to get tweets directed at them, it is like public praise that everyone of your followers will see also. They may even pick up a few followers from you, if they tweet you back then all their followers will see your username and you could pick up followers if they check out your profile and find you and the conversation interesting. Tweeting is a team sport not a solo activity, so join the conversation, answer your tweets and show that you are an interactive twitter user, this will get you more followers.

The other way to communicate on twitter is the direct message. While still confined to 140 characters direct messages can be used by either clicking the envelope by a user or going under the message tab, direct messages are private and not seen by anyone but you and the receiver. These are used for private conversations. I use them to talk to my twitter friends directly about things that only concern the two of us. If I ask another author for a blurb for the back cover of one of my books I don't want to put them on the spot in front of the whole twitterverse that is bad etiquette. So that is a private message. One of my twitter friends who is a portfolio manager asked me to call him by sending me a direct message with his phone number, he did not want my thousands of followers at the time to all have his personal phone number so it was a private direct message. I also use direct messages for private conversations that our followers would not be interested in.

It is important that private conversations are kept private, and you build trust and friendship with interesting people on twitter. It is also important that you interact with people in your own tweet timeline. So just do what fits your personality decide how public or private each conversation should be and keep it that way.

8. Followers to following ratio

Do you know how to make your twitter profile really unappealing? Follow the maximum people allowed right from the start. Who wants to follow a user that shows this on their profile?

0	2,002	0	0
Tweets	Following	Followers	Listed

This looks like a desperate spammer not someone that people will be drawn to follow. In all likelihood if you are lucky you will end up with some reciprocal follows from people who follow everyone back. Unfortunately it is unlikely anyone will really want to read your tweets. It is much better to start out slow and follow maybe 100 people that tweet about what you are most interested in. Following a 100 people or less is a good place to start out. Use that as a place to start and read others tweets and reply to them.

This will look much better to potential followers.

23	100	25	1
Tweets	Following	Followers	Listed

If you decide to only follow people that will follow you back and your account shows an almost equal ratio of follower to follow you will attract the follow back crowd. This can be good to pick up followers but bad because many people will follow you back for the sole person of getting another follower themselves with no intention to ever read any of your tweets. You will have no way of knowing how many "real" followers you have. At the same time some real followers will not follow anyone unless they receive a follow back in return. We will discuss this further later in the book.

23	100	100	1
Tweets	Following	Followers	Listed

Some people consider the most attractive twitter accounts to have a huge amount of followers compared to the amount of people they are following. This shows potential followers that you are interesting and people are engaged. Profiles with 10 to 1 or 100 to 1 ratios of more followers than who they follow really show people that are looking at your account that you are a twitter pro. This is the most attractive account appearance to attract real followers. Oddly enough other real followers will not follow anyone that does not follow back. They believe that unless you are a superstar you should follow everyone back and be twitter "friends".

193	100	1023	23
Tweets	Following	Followers	Listed

So I would just say be mindful of how your following to follower ratio looks on twitter, do not follow too many accounts too quickly, and do not look like a spammer. Do not look desperate for followers, just build your account systematically with daily interesting tweets, and follow people that are interesting. Follow back people that you really find interesting or follow everyone back, it is your choice. Keep your ratios pretty balanced, don't get carried away and follow too many people to fast.

9. No spamming

**Spam –noun 2. (lowercase) disruptive messages, espe-
cially commercial messages posted on a computer network
or sent as e-mail. –Dictionary.com (Used with permission.)**

Twitter rule #1 no spamming, rule #2 never forget rule #1.
If you have been chosen to be followed because you have kept
your tweet stream full of quality tweets do not run that follower off by having a weak moment of desperate spamming.

If it is the end of the month and you are three sales away
from making your goal of 100 sales from your affiliate account, go take a cold shower. Do not stoop to sending out
your affiliate link 100 times in one day. This will make your
followers know not to click your link because they have already seen it, over and over. The worst part is by resorting
to spam you either make your real followers stop looking at
your tweets permanently or worse even make them unfollow
you altogether.

If you want to have a successful twitter account that attracts and keeps followers then only use affiliate accounts
when they are tied into conversations or you are sending
them after a useful tweet.

Exhibit A: When you review a product on Amazon.com
and tweet out your Amazon affiliate link to that product an-
nouncing you have reviewed it, and give your opinion, that
is appropriate.

Exhibit B: Sending out a pay per click pharmaceutical link
nine times throughout the day and you mainly tweet about
sports as your main topic, that is inappropriate and will turn
away followers.

There are far too many twitter accounts to follow for any
follower to put up with inappropriate spam. Your job is to

provide great content if you want 1000 followers on twitter. You should not even be aiming for twitter income until you have built up several hundred followers and are established. Take a page out of Mark Zuckerberg's playbook: he focused on growth first and then income when building facebook.

Also do not spam followers through direct messages. That is very bad manners on twitter. Direct messages are for connecting with people on a personal level, not secretly spamming them behind all your followers back. If you are on twitter with the purpose of generating future income then you should realize that all great sales people build a relationship with their customers, and then customers buy because they trust the sales person. The products should also live up to the recommendation given so you turn your followers into repeat customers, if that is your goal.

Income generation links should be imbedded in your high quality tweet stream, not sticking out like a sore thumb.

10. Listed?

How do you separate yourself from the millions of other twitter users? Get listed. You will make your twitter account look more attractive if you have been added to other user's lists.

345	1026	1021	23
Tweets	Following	Followers	Listed

Lists are created by twitter users to separate twitter accounts into categories. For the most part people use lists to separate the very best twitter users from the rest. Someone might be following 350 accounts on twitter, but list 12 of those in a list called "Most Interesting" now if they are running short on time they can just look at the tweet stream for those 12 accounts instead of the what all 350 accounts are tweeting about. Also other users can follow your list if you have created one that is interesting or informative.

The key is that if someone sees your profile and you are not listed at all, it could make some people believe you are not as interesting as others. How do you get listed? By providing great tweets, and making friends. Some people also will list you if you are tweeting about a specialized topic they are interested in. You can also create lists for your favorites. Some of them may reciprocate and list you back.

Being listed is like a reward for providing great content. Not only is someone following you, but they think you are so interesting, educational, inspirational, or funny that they are separating you into a list to make sure they do not miss your tweets. That is a high complement, and one you have to earn. When you achieve this it will make your profile more attractive to followers. The more lists you are added to the better.

(Note: A user can list you without following you).

PART II
Provide Great Content

11. What's happening?

That is the question above our tweet box on our home page: What's happening? Answer this question with your audience in mind. If you only have 11 followers and they are all your personal friends then by all means tweet the small stuff.

> "I am eating breakfast and going to the mall in about an hour, who wants to go?"

They may be wondering what you are doing and may want to get together later. That is a valid use of twitter and why many people do not use it. Most people do not care about the minutiae of others lives. So if you want twenty followers tweet the small stuff. **If you want 1000 followers then you will need to tweet things that are informative, interesting, interactive, or funny.**

Here are some better examples:

Informative:

> "Did you know breakfast means to break the fast? This is what we do in the morning we eat after fasting for 8 to 10 hours."

Interesting:

> "Did you know 100% bran cereal with strawberries only has 200 calories and fills me up every morning?"

Funny:

> "After breakfast I will continue my quest for 1000 followers, if you know where follower number 892 is please let me know, I am looking for them."

Interactive:

> "My favorite cereal is 100% bran with strawberries in whole milk, what's yours?"

Tweeting about what's happening is an art form, put

thought into it; bring your personality in, tweet about who you are and what you are interested in. The above examples may be too personal if you are tweeting for a business, but may be perfect if you are tweeting about health or weight loss. Figure out who you want your key audience to be and create tweets that target their interests, which should mainly be your own.

Your followers are following you for these updates, be sure that you put thought into each one. Tell about interesting things that are happening to you.

1. You met a famous person.
2. You sent a manuscript to a publisher.
3. You saw a great movie that you loved.
4. You read an excellent book.
5. You took a class and learned something new.
6. There is breaking news in your city that has not gone national yet.
7. You lost weight on a new diet.
8. You have a blog update.
9. You wrote an Amazon.com review.
10. You posted on your facebook fan page.

The above are examples of things that followers like to hear about, I am sure you can think of many more. Make your tweets useful and stay away from useless ones.

Don't tweet the small stuff.

12. Use the 'add this' tool bar

Twitter is a great form of communication because you have the ability to share anything you find interesting on the web by tweeting the link out, but you can't copy and paste a huge link into your 140 character tweet without taking up all the room you need to comment on it. The solution is the quickest and easiest way to share online that I have seen is to add a toolbar from the website: http://www.addthis.com/.

Addthis is the world's largest content sharing and social insights platform. It has easy-to-use tools that help users to share their content and drive viral traffic on the web. This service enables users to install an 'addthis' toolbar to their web browser that allows the user to share content with the push of a button on almost any social media website. After you download the toolbar from addthis.com you have the ability to see a great article on a blog about the topic you are interested in and just push the twitter button on the tool bar and share the article with all your followers. You just have to keep your twitter account signed in to make it as easy as pushing a button. You may also want to add in your thoughts about the link or delete the 'via addthis' note on the end of the tweet. The great thing is it creates a short website url on the tweet so you have room to add your thoughts and opinions. In the past people had to go to a site and enter the full website url to get a shortened url to use, now it is only one click.

Through add this you can share:
1. Blog articles by yourself or others.
2. News from web sites.
3. Your facebook fan page.
4. Your website.
5. Link to purchase a newsletter.

6. Your Amazon.com reviews.

7. Your facebook profile.

8. Your MySpace profile.

9. Your LinkedIn profile.

10. Popular youtube videos.

These are just ten of many ideas that you can use. With the addthis toolbar you can literally share anything you find interesting while surfing the web with your followers with one click.

If you are trying to drive traffic to the link then you should have an interesting tweet along with the link you are sharing.

If you want to tweet out your favorite diet book then the addthis twitter button will give you an automatic tweet that looks like this:

> "Amazon.com: Why We Get Fat: And What to Do About It (9780307272706): Gary Taubes: Books: http://amzn.to/jHU4i9 via @addthis"

To make it a more interesting tweet you could delete all the information except for the url and tweet out:

> "How I lost 50 pounds in three months>>>>> http://amzn.to/jHU4i9"

This could peak some interest if weight loss and health is what you tweet about. Or if your followers know you recently lost weight.

Another tweet could be:

> "One diet book that really works, two thumbs up! Why We Get Fat: And What to Do About It: Gary Taubes: Books: http://amzn.to/jHU4i9"

Do not over do it with links, have a good mix of links and just tweets along with replies to others tweets. Send out a good ratio of interesting tweets that you are not affiliated with and mix in a few of your own to fan pages, blogs, and websites. If you over due tweeting out your own links your followers will likely quit clicking any of your links. Updating them on new posts though will keep them informed.

Tweet out links that are informative, interesting, entertaining, and educational to keep your followers coming back for more.

13. Tweet your opinions

People like to hear endorsements for things from ordinary people. If there are ten 5 star reviews for a book on Amazon they are more likely to trust those ten reviews from random people than a paid ad in a magazine telling how great the book is.

If you tell your followers that you loved a recent movie you went to see that will likely influence their decision more to go see it than the movie trailers. In the age of Social Media people go to amazon.com, facebook, and twitter to get others opinions before spending their hard earned money.

When you develop a relationship with your followers and even many become friends your opinion will matter to them. You may have strong opinions about your area of interest. You may be a movie buff who has watched thousands of movies. When you list your top ten movie favorites of all time your followers will listen. You may even inspire DVD sales or sale movie tickets after you tweet a positive review. (It is good to always provide a link along with your recommendation to the source you recommend buying from also. Followers like to save time.) If they end up enjoying the movie just like you predicted then you may become their source for recommendations. This could inspire them to tweet you and ask you what your favorite drama was, or comedy, this is what creates robust twitter accounts that start transforming into informational hubs in Social Media. If others chime in their favorites then you are really on the right track.

So share your favorites in your area of interest. Tweet why you love that item. Also share your dislikes so you do not look like a paid pumper. Be respectful in why you dislike an item do not take it to a place where you are a troll just attacking things because you have a negative streak. The internet respects clearly stated opinions not paid pumpers or completely negative trolls that attack everything.

Let your followers know what you like and dislike and why.

14. Tweet Jokes

If you can make someone laugh in 140 characters or less, by all means do it. If you read a tweet that makes you laugh retweet it. If you can sprinkle in entertainment and laughter into your tweet stream that will go a long way to getting and keeping followers.

Almost everyone loves a good sense of humor. As long as you keep your jokes tasteful this well add another great element to your twitter account.

What are some good rules for jokes? If it makes you laugh then it is likely to make others laugh. Puns, sarcasm, your making fun of yourself, pointing out the ridiculous in a situation are all things that many find funny.

You will know if your joke was funny by the replies and retweets, if all you here are crickets chirping after the tweet then it is likely you missed the mark.

"Laughter is the closest distance between two people." –Victor Borge

15. Tweet Great Quotes

In all my tweeting and posting on facebook I have learned without any doubt that people love inspirational quotes. Inspirational quotes were like tweets throughout history. Great quotes capture thoughts, teachings, principles, and inspiration and most times in 140 characters or less. Great quotes are perfect for using on twitter, especially if you can find ones that match the subject matter you are tweeting about.

One of my main topic areas is the stock market and stock trading so tweets that are quotes from successful money managers and traders are received very well. Many times a quote from a successful person will capture a principle in a form that is very compatible with twitter. I am always careful to name who the quote is from to give proper credit. You do not want to get caught as a twitter plagiarist from someone familiar with a quote. Always give credit where credit is due.

Any simple Google of the word "quotes" will give you all the material you could want. You should add an additional name to be more specific about what you are looking for. A Green Bay Packer fan on twitter may want to Google "Vince Lombardi quotes" if his team is approaching the playoffs. While a twitter account about value stock investing may tweet out a Warren Buffett quote almost daily.

Your job is to pick out the best ones that tie into your subject area and that are from people related to your topics. People love quotes that inspire them by giving them a principle that will make them more successful. Or a quote that really sums up a deep held belief that most people have. Just be sure the quote you pick is the right one and it matches your tweet stream. They are great for clarifying and giving authority to something you are trying to convey.

Great quotes from historical figures are like tweets from the past.

16. Tweet great pictures (twitpics)

Do you have a great picture or image you would like to share? You can sign up with the web site http://twitpic.com/ using your twitter account and share pictures and images with your followers. It is very simple and easy to use. You will have your own profile page on twitpics that contains all your down loads. You will have the ability to tweet them out with comments. Others can also leave comments on the web site with their thoughts about your down loaded images. You will see the amount of views that you get for each posted picture or image.

This is a great tool to use to make your tweet stream more interesting. When people click onto your tweets on their home page they will be able to see the image in your tweet in the right hand column on twitter. This could draw people to click your image and keep followers interested.

I use twitpic to download and share images of book covers that I have before they are released to the public. Followers like to get an early look at what will be released soon and feel informed before the general public. By itself it is a small thing but added with all the other sources of information it adds value to your twitter account.

You can use twitpic to share comics, graphs, charts, photos, drawings, and anything visual that ties into your tweet topics. This is a great tool to add to your twitter account; you get an image and can tweet with the characters left over from the link.

A picture is worth a thousand characters.

17. Tweet breaking news

If you are at the scene of some breaking news and you have your cell phone you can scoop all the news agencies. Hopefully it will not be something tragic. In the age of twitter this has happened, people tweet out what is going on while they are there, in other countries it is the latest news in political upheavals that are tweeted out before the service is cut off. In the U.S. tweets come out in storm ravaged areas. In the age of social media it is possible for someone to take pictures on the scene, download to twitpics and share with their followers on twitter.

Hopefully though, you will simply be sharing breaking news that you hear locally that has not made the national news yet. A local coach of a professional team has resigned. Or your state legislature has just passed a major bill and it is on the local news. This is a time you can go off topic for the sake of sharing information you have before others.

I also like to tweet and comment on huge events like when Osama Bin Laden was found. If you are right there on twitter when the news breaks and you tweet it out, in the age of social media YOU may be the place your followers hear it from first. In the second decade of the 21st century many televisions are left off and many people, especially the younger generation get their news from the internet instead of television and radio.

Be sure to always tweet out and start conversations about the headlines that concern your main topic area. Users who focus on sports need to comment on major events in the sports world, stock traders need to comment on stock market news, and health experts need to focus on new studies about health from the medical field.

Do not tweet in a bubble, incorporate what is going on in the world into your tweets. This also helps with interaction. Many people would like to discuss major events and how they affect the world.

Stay current, keep yourself relevant, be a source for breaking news.

18. Tweet your favorite books

If you have some favorite books about your topic area, then share them. Find them on amazon.com, BarnesandNoble.cm, or Booksamillion.com and tweet them out to your followers using addthis. Be sure to edit the tweet and tell your followers why you like the book. They will be able to click on your link and go directly to the book. I would suggest always provide a link to the product you are recommending, people do not want to have to go look it up, the odds are they will not.

If they do decide to buy the book you recommend and they love it, then you have built credibility with that follower. In the future they will be likely to follow your future recommendations. This is how you build a true social media presence, one good experience at a time.

Amazon.com does have an affiliate account where you can actually earn commissions when people click your links and make a purchase. The commission percentage grows as you sell more products through your links. You can go ahead and sign up for this but I would not make any attempts to truly monetize your tweets until you have 1000 followers. Unless of course your twitter account is about book reviewing, video gaming, or electronics and you will be discussing products as the major part of your timeline. Then it may benefit you from the beginning because you would be sending product links anyway.

Sharing books is a great way to inform your followers. If you have read fifty or one hundred books in your area of interest and can point to the five best then you are providing a useful service that your followers will appreciate.

You can also tweet out books to avoid, explain exactly what a specific book could teach a follower, and if you have your own book you could tweet out a blurb quote endorsing it or a nugget of wisdom found in it.

With the book industry changing so fast you need to consider whether your audience prefers physical books, kindle editions, or Nook. If you interact you will find out.

19. Review Movies

If you have gone to see a recently released movie or watched one that has just become available for home then you could share your opinions with your followers. If you tweet about sports and it is a new movie about sports then that is perfect. If you tweet about the stock market and you are tweeting about a newly released movie about Wall Street that is also perfect.

Ideally you want to watch and tweet about movies on their first week of release before your followers have had a chance to watch them. It is pretty irrelevant to tweet about a movie that has been at the theaters for a month and is not released to view at home yet. It is also irrelevant if a movie has been released for home viewing through DVD or On Demand for two months then you give your opinion. The odds are that your followers have already seen it. So you need to be a first mover if you want to be a relevant tweeter about movies you have seen.

Once again if you see a movie the first weekend of its release and you tweet about how great it is, then your follower goes to see it because of your recommendation and also loves it then you build credibility with your audience. If they send you a public tweet thanking you that also builds your credibility with their followers.

If you are a movie buff and your twitter account is about movies then reviews about movies when they are released may be the main thing you do. In that case you will really need to go see movies the day they are released and be the very first person to tweet your opinions both positive and negative. This will really help you become the source for many followers to get your feedback on movie before anyone else has even gone to see it.

You can also post a written review for a movie on sites like Yahoo! or Amazon.com and tweet out a link to your review so you can fully express yourself without the limit of 140 characters. You can add your twitter user name on your profile at these other web sites also so people that really enjoy your reviews can follow you on twitter.

20. Review television shows

With the vast sea of television programs that are now showing on the hundreds of cable and satellite networks, who wouldn't want a recommendation? It would even be helpful to know which shows to watch on a specific channel that runs 24 hour content. Some sports fans would like to know if they are missing any great shows on the Golf Channel or the NFL channel. There may even be a show on one of the sports channels about a followers' specific interest that they may not even be aware of.

The key is to share your favorites with your followers or even a great tidbit of information that was shared on one of the shows you like watching. If you tweet about the stock market you could share your opinion about the top five financial news networks and which ones you find most informative and which ones are biased. You can also tweet out your top five favorite shows and why you like them. This could stir conversations with followers which is an added bonus.

It is okay to mix in some personal likes and dislikes in your tweet stream to make your account feel more personal. You could tweet about the first episode of a new show on the major networks and whether it was entertaining and who it might appeal to. You could give your opinion about a shows cancellation. You could also share something that you learned from watching a show that is about your topic area that you did not know.

Your tweets could be a lighthouse in an ocean of television programming leading your followers to quality broadcasts that they will enjoy.

PART III

Are you an expert? Then share your knowledge.

21. Most people are an expert on something

Is there anything that you just can't stop talking about? Is there a topic that everyone around you just gets tired of hearing about over and over again? Do you wake up excited about the same thing every day and just can't wait to get started in it and see what's going on? Have you purposely or accidentally spent thousands of hours doing something and getting better and better at it to a point where you have started giving advice to your friends and family and it works? If you have an answer to these questions then that is what you should be tweeting about.

The reason real followers will follow a person on twitter is to read tweets about the topics they are interested in. They want to be informed on what is currently going on, they want to learn from someone who has more experience and know more than they do.

Your topic could be computers, web sites, electronics, smart phones, video games, books, movies, social media, stock trading, investing, business, success, inspiration, sports or whatever you are passionate about.

Some followers are well versed in the topic and may just follow you to have someone to tweet with or share their opinions with. This is also great for networking and you may learn from those you are connecting with on twitter. If you get enough followers around your topic of interest you will be able to have your own questions answered by tweeting out a question.

So think about what you spend the majority of your time doing and talking about, you may be an expert and not even know it. Also your family and friends will be glad you have an outlet to express yourself so they can get a rest from listening. Your followers will also be glad that you shared your knowledge and experience.

22. Sell yourself

Why should anyone follow you? You should sell yourself in your bio and tweets.

If you are tweeting about stock trading and have beat the S&P 500 for six straight years then put it in your bio. If you are tweeting about a video game and you hold a world ranking in one, then put it on your bio. If you're tweeting out your reviews from Amazon. com and you are a top 100 helpful reviewer then tell your followers how you got that ranking. You need to ad credibility to your voice to really get followers to listen to what you have to say.

Other twitter users have let their quality tweets sell the account to their followers. If you tweet out several will constructed, clever, informative, and entertaining tweets each day that will also sell your account.

If you recommendations are good and followers like the products you recommend then you are building your followers trust that your judgment is good.

If you recommend a stock and it goes up in value and your followers make money then you are selling your stock picking abilities.

If your tweets are retweeted by 20 of your followers you are selling yourself as a great tweet writer.

If your followers are sending you public messages about how you helped them or how they loved your book or product then that is you selling yourself as someone to be followed.

You need to be consistent with your tweets, tweet at regular times almost every day. Send out only great tweets do not get lazy or over tweet so they lose their quality. Think about the products you are recommending. Always be truthful. When you are successful at something tweet about your successes without being arrogant, just be informative.

Also present yourself as someone that has information to share and is an authority in their tweet topic because of experience and past successes.

23. Share your reviews

Do you write reviews on the web? If you write reviews on Amazon.com or other sites then that is something that would be great to tweet out after it is posted.

You could tweet out first that you are trying to decide what you are going to purchase, tweeting out different items you are trying to choose from. Your followers may chime in with recommendations. Interaction would be a great bonus. Then you could tweet out that you have made the purchase and are looking forward to checking out the product when it arrives. (You should provide a link to the specific item.) Then after you have used the item and wrote a review you could tweet out the product with a link to your review explaining in a tweet whether you liked it or not. Which hopefully will lead to further interaction, if not you will be informing your followers of your opinions. This could help them make decisions on whether they want to purchase the item or not.

This is a great use of twitter for top reviewers on Amazon.com. Reviews are the main things that they do. Some specialize in electronics, health, or book reviews in a specific genre. Twitter is a natural extension to what they are already doing. Twitter enables top reviewers to tweet out their own personal opinions and thoughts and they do not always have to be captured inside a review. Twitter will set serial reviewers free to micro-blog their thoughts along with their reviews.

So, if you are already reviewing, share them with your followers. If not, you may want to start reviewing items that tie in with your tweeting topic or your blog if you have one. These are items you will be using anyway so why not share your opinions?

Video gamers can write reviews on the accessories they use while playing, stock traders can review brokers, financial television shows, and stock market books. There are products about whatever your topic area is on twitter that you could review.

This is a great way to add informative content to your tweets that are about your topic area. Some of us are already writing them we just have to tweet them.

24. Know your audience

Who is your target twitter audience? Do you want to appeal to everyone? If you are tweeting inspirational quotes, self-help, or news then that may be possible. However if you are tweeting about the stock market then you need to target a specific audience, will it be day traders, long term investors, growth investors, value investors, or trend traders? Will it be targeted at new traders or experienced traders? Will you be giving stock tips or teaching traders how to trade? **You need to aim for a target audience or you may end up with no audience.**

You need to tweet with your audience in mind. Do not send out tweets that insult your followers intelligence if you are aiming for a higher level of experience in your topic area, and do not tweet over their heads if you are trying to teach something on twitter. You want to make an effort to make your tweets on target for your audience.

How will you know if you are doing a good job? Followers will retweet your best tweets to share them with others. You will not lose followers, you will gain followers. Your followers will recommend others follow you publicly through tweets. You will be listed by others in your topic area with other great twitter accounts. That is how you know you are winning and doing a good job.

However if you are continually losing followers, you get no retweets, and no listings or recommendations you are off the mark. You need to go look at how other successful twitter users are managing their accounts or read this book one more time and follow the recommendations.

Tweet what you love, share your favorite websites and blogs with your followers. What would they find interesting?

What could you inform them about that they do not already know? What would be funny and amusing to tweet? Do you give back praise and retweets to others? Do you over do it on the affiliate links or selling? Is it worth following you and reading all your tweets?

Only you know the answers to these questions. If you are not getting the results you expected then you need to honestly answer these questions.

25. Share all your favorite books

I have found it interesting to suggest books along with answers to specific questions around my area of experience. I use to do this on e-mail but now I find 140 characters with a book link can lead the person to an answer better than I can without typing out a term paper length response.

I also have enjoyed creating tweets that count down my favorite ten books along a topic area. I personally have read around one thousand books so I have no trouble with top ten lists on just about any subject. But most people have favorite fiction books or fiction authors they can tweet out.

If you tweet about relationships then you could tweet out the top ten books that will help followers find the perfect mate.

How to books are also popular.

If you tweet about personal finance then this would be a great tweet around tax time:

> This book helped me this year. If you want to do your own income taxes then read (BOOK LINK HERE)

If you can direct followers to a book that solves a problem that they have, that you have overcome then you are truly helping them.

> Here is how I finally quit smoking (BOOK LINK HERE)

Share books that have changed your life.
Share books that have influenced you to be successful.
Share books that have taught you something valuable.
Share books that are funny and entertaining.
Also, don't forget to ask your followers for their favorites.

26. Share career knowledge

If you have been a successful butcher, baker, or candle-stick maker, then there are people that would appreciate your knowledge and tips. While in the 21st century some success-ful careers that will attract followers are personal trainers, chefs, and web site designers.

There are people very interested in learning about things like cooking, weight loss, and website design among many other things. For professionals twitter could just be an ex-tension of their business. It could even get your name out there to a wide audience and even generate customers, sales, and business. That has been my experience as an author. I have made some great contacts through twitter to people I would have never met in day to day life. I have learned from them and they have helped tremendously with my published books. So if you tweet about your area of interest and stay with it, inevitably you will run across and connect with oth-ers of like minds and it could lead to business and projects.

If you have been successful in a field that can translate to twitter then you can share your principles of success and your experiences with those trying to make it in your field. Whether it is web sites, publishing, management, investing, or education there are real followers that really want to hear what you have to say. They need your knowledge and know how. If you have had a successful career do not underestimate how valuable your mentoring may be to someone starting out in the field.

If you are in a field that many others want to break into and the competition is intense like music, acting, publishing, trad-ing, or entertainment and you have reached a level of success that they want, you may be surprised at how quickly you pick up followers that will be engaged in reading your tweets. You may have the keys to the career that they want to take for a test drive.

27. Share your blog posts

Twitter is a great tool to use if you write a blog. Some people have twitter accounts for no other purpose than to push their blogs out to a larger audience. While twitter is a micro-blog it can be used as a satellite for a full size blog. You can use the 140 character tweet to create interest in the full size posting that it was inspired from.

One of the primary uses of twitter is to drive traffic. By having a twitter account to compliment your blog, people will stumble upon your twitter then see your blog link that they probably would have never even known existed.

I am able to drive hundreds of views to my facebook fan page after a few tweets, while if I simply wrote an entry and left it at that it is likely I would only get five to ten views from people that stumble upon it from web searches or randomly.

You want the tweet to be interesting and raise curiosity in the follower.

A tweet like:

"How to sell more of your books on Amazon (Inserted Link)"

May get a yawn from your followers, but a tweet like this:

"I just sold 500 copies of my book in 90 days this is how>>>>(Inserted Link)"

Of course the amount of trust and relationships you have built will come into play on whether your followers click the link. If you can back up your tweet with a very useful blog post that really works you are on your road to success in tweeting. The key is when they click to your blog that you fill a need, solve a problem, inform, or educate, if you do that they can't help but to come back for more.

With all the ways you can use to promote your twitter account it is likely that you can bring your blog traffic up a great deal from having a twitter account properly promoted like we will discuss in this book.

One thousand engaged followers could result in hundreds more that read your blog posts and may eventually follow your blog.

In the time of social media it is crucial that all bloggers have a twitter account just to keep up with others.

A blogger without a twitter account is like a car without an engine.

28. Share interesting facts

Do you tweet about movies and know the only action movie that had two future governors in lead roles? Then tweet it. (Predator: Arnold Schwarzenegger and Jesse Ventura.) Do you tweet about the stock market and just realize the stock market went down for the 6th straight day and that the market has only gone down 6 times in a row 45 times since 1928? Time to tweet out those interesting facts.

Sharing interesting facts about your area of knowledge or expertise is entertaining and adds credibility to your tweets. If you can tweet out facts that are little known but true that really stick with your followers they may very well remember that you are where they heard it from. So when they use the fact to impress friends they know who gave them the tidbit of information and will likely come back for more.

People that tweet about sports have an ample amount of statistics and facts to tweet about. Most of us if we have spent thousands of hours doing something or studying it have many interesting things we have learned that can be shared.

If you know of something that you do that doubles the amount of people that visit your web site share it.

If you tweet about health and you know one thing that helps you lose weight then let your followers know. We all know of some interesting facts that we can share with our followers. Let's share them.

When we are surfing the web, reading an interesting article or book, reading other tweets, or our facebook news feed and we stumble upon an interesting fact that relates to our tweet topic, let's not be selfish, tweet it out.

29. Share specialized knowledge

Do you know how to cook the perfect pot roast and you tweet about cooking? Are you a lawyer and can walk someone through the steps to write a will? Are you a website designer who can tweet out how someone can build their own web site in 30 steps?

Doctors, lawyers, computer programmers, nutritionists, personal trainers, money managers, and many other professionals have specialized knowledge on how to do things that the vast majority of people do not. Followers may be following you for hints, tips, and the know how to do things they cannot do on their own but you know how.

A nutritionist may be able to tweet about changes in eating habits that will really help you lose weight. They may know because they have helped many clients lose weight. This is not just their opinion that is what they have a degree in and do every day. Followers will sit up and listen.

But you do not necessarily have to be a professional. You may be a master of a popular online video game and be ranked as one of the best in the world. You may be able to explain how to get to a difficult level or how to rank higher by doing certain things.

On twitter anything you have accomplished you can help others to accomplish. If you are a published author you can give others steps to use and advice on how to also be a published author. If you have a website in the top 1% of all websites in the world then you have the right to tweet with authority to others on how to do what you did. They may also tweet you with questions and learn from you. That is the great thing about twitter, knowledge sharing on an epic scale. **On twitter you can help others have the same level of success that you have had.** (You should also follow people that are where you want to be, that share how they did it.)

30. Share your life lessons

If you have accomplished great things then you probably have a few lessons that you have learned along the way. You may not even be aware of what you know until you realize someone else is making a mistake that you did in the past.

A life lesson may come to you in the middle of the work day when you see a peer that is going down the wrong road. You may see someone on television or the web that has ruined their life and a life lesson pops in your head that the person should have followed to avoid their grief. It is also possible that you stumble upon a quote that sums up a lesson that you know to be true. Well what do you do when these thoughts pop in your head? You tweet them!

> "Winners are simply those who never quit."

> "You have to work really hard for a very long time to get lucky."

> "Passion, perseverance, and hard work=success."

> "Too many of us are looking for a job, paycheck, or a career, what we really need is a passion, a mission, a quest worthy of our efforts."

I am sure some really great ones have also come to your mind. The ones that come from your heart are the best ones. I have received a lot of retweets for great life lessons that came from my own personal experience, they really resonate with people and sometimes it is really what they need to hear on a particular day to keep them on their path in life.

Try to avoid old ones that have been so over used that they have become clichés. Try to tweet out lessons that you have learned the hard way and you know in your heart to be true from personal experience.

Share the lessons you have learned in your topic area specifically or life in general, they could be helpful to others. Or they could just agree with a "Yes that is so true!" Either way it is all good.

PART IV
Getting your name out there

31. Top tweeters

So you are just a tweeting away. You follow a few interesting people and you have a few followers. You tweet and tweet, (crickets chirping.) and tweet some more. A week later you have 7 followers. You are sad. How can you get more followers? You have an attractive profile, you are an expert on your topic, and you have some great content. What is a good way for people to find you?

If you go to http://twitaholic.com/ you can see the top 1000 accounts on twitter and how many followers each account currently has. I recommend following a hundred of these top 1000 accounts that are on the topic you are interested in. If you tweet about music then you can follow the top 100 singers. What this does is make it easier for other music lovers to find you. If you are following Lady Gaga, Taylor Swift, and Katy Perry then you increase your odds of showing up on other accounts under the 'who to follow' suggestions. Also many people look at the followers of their favorite accounts to find other people to follow. If you tweet under @Gaga-Fan2011 and follow @ladygaga and she has almost eleven million followers then you have a lot of chances of other fans finding you. If you throw in some messages and retweets to her account then you have a very good chance of likeminded people finding you and following and really wanting to hear about their favorite singer.

You should only follow the top 100 accounts that relate to your topic, if you are tweeting about professional basketball then you would not follow Lady Gaga even though she is the most popular, that will not help you. You would follow Shaq, the NBA, the Los Angeles Lakers and all the other accounts that relate to what you are tweeting about. This will do a few things:

1. Increase the odds of being followed by others who are also following several of the same accounts by being suggested to them on 'who to follow'.

2. People could follow you when they are searching the followers of their favorite accounts.

3. You get your account profile out there for more people to see that would not have seen it and show them that you are interested in the same thing they are.

Do not be an island, who you follow says a lot about what your account is all about, especially in the early stages of building it.

Take your time to search the top 1000 accounts to find at least one hundred that you really are interested in and plan to keep up with. This is a win-win and a great way to boost you account and get it seen by others on twitter.

32. Interesting people

Now that you have a nice tweet stream you can sit and watch it. You will see interesting tweets flow by on your home page. Now you want to find interesting people to follow. They can be found through interactions with accounts you are following. If you see and interesting retweet, then click the original sender and read their tweets. If they are interesting then follow them. Reply and interact to tweets that you have an opinion about or just want to say you like it or agree with it. You will get your best use out of twitter by interacting with interesting people. You not only build relationships through interaction but a lot of the time you attract the other person's followers to follow you. Generally the people you find interesting are likeminded with your interests. This is how networks are built on twitter. **People with like minds connect through sharing information.**

The most important thing you can do is mingle on twitter, interact, complement, and share. Adding an additional one hundred people that you find very interesting will also bring up the quality of your tweet stream. You can learn from them and they could be a source for articles and information that you retweet to bring up the quality of your own tweets.

Creating a list called "Interesting People" and listing them could also give you brownie points with them and show you really like their contributions. This could result in them retweeting you and interacting with your tweets.

Finding and following interesting people on twitter is great fun, enjoy the search.

33. Tweets you want to read

Now with your home tweet stream swelling to over 200 sources of information you may have to start making decisions on exactly how you will manage all this inflow of information. If you do not have 10 free hours a day to sit and read all the tweets you may have to start dividing and conquering this tidal wave of useful tweets.

One suggestion I have is to create lists. One could be your top ten twitter account that you want to read every day for their knowledge and information. You could title it "my favorites" or "Best tweets on twitter" this will complement the people with the accounts at the same time you are dividing the tidal wave into manageable streams. Now if you are pushed for time on a certain day instead of trying to swim the raging river of the tweets on your home page or search and find your favorites one at a time, you click your list and read the tweets, comment, reply, or just learn something new and then move on with your day. This also ensures you do not miss out on a vital tweet from your favorite must read tweeters.

Other tweets that you do not want to miss out on are from your friends, family, or twitter network. Your friends or family lists are pretty self explanatory, and it is obvious what you should name those lists and then decide how often you should check in on their tweets.

Your twitter network is a little different. I believe that it is important to show reciprocation after you receive a compliment, listing, or retweet. This is a way you build a real following. If you receive a retweet then that proves to you that the person is really reading your tweets. (Or at least they read that one tweet). This is your chance to either thank them with a public message, or list them in a list like 'My network' or 'My retweeters' while you are showing gratitude which is always great because people like to feel appreciated you are also creating a way that you can follow up and possibly retweet a tweet of theirs in the future. This is a great way to build followers because they know that they also have a follower so they are more inclined to continue to follow you to see if you retweet them again.

Under my network I list all the authors who have given me blurbs for books, shout outs I received and my facebook friends that are on twitter that I have interacted with on various projects.

It is important to read the tweets from the members of your network and people that are show interest in what you are doing.

Managing your account so you do not miss opportunities to connect and grow your influence and show your real followers you care about what they are doing.

34. Retweets

All twitter users need to be monitoring their home page under the retweets tab daily. By clicking this tab you can see if you had any tweets retweeted. By clicking the tweet itself you can see in the right column on your home page who has retweeted one of your tweets. This is very important information to have if you want to know who your real followers are and interact with them.

A retweet is one of the best compliments you can receive on twitter. When someone retweets they are:

1. Endorsing someone else's tweet to their followers.

2. Saying that their followers should click the link, if there is one.

3. Advertising the original tweeter as someone that could be followed.

4. Broadcasting that they are reading the tweets of that account.

5. Showing that they really liked that tweet.

Daily retweets show you that you are providing quality tweets to your followers and that they are reading what you have to say. Repeated retweets from the same person shows that they may be reading all of your tweets. You really need to respond with thanks and retweets of their best tweets. You need to always give back on twitter and show you appreciate the interest. Participating with your audience is crucial to keep their interest. Do not just broadcast, this is not television it is more like sending telegrams back and forth publicly. After retweets, send out public thanks when it seems appropriate.

Retweets come from sending quality tweets to an engaged audience. If your tweets are informative, interactive, entertaining, or interesting and people are reading them you will get retweets. If you have lost your audience through neglect and then have a great tweet then no one will read it and there will be no retweets. If you do have people reading your tweets but they are not great then you will have no retweets.

A retweet happens when a great tweet meets a follower who loves it. Retweets can really gauge the quality of your tweets and the engagement of your audience.

They are the best advertisements to get more followers and move toward your goal of 1000 real followers.

If a great tweet is tweeted on twitter and no one is there to read it, does it make a difference?

35. @Comments

Interactions are what you should be spending the majority of your time doing on twitter not broadcasting endless tweets. The best way to interact is publicly by using the @ symbol followed by the username that your comment is directed at. You use this function to give your opinion, ask a question, answer a question, thank someone for a retweet or shout out along with just plain conversation about a topic you are both interested in. A lot of times a tweet will start a conversation, sometimes it grows and others join with their perspectives and thoughts. These can turn into very good ways to connect with followers. Sometimes a long conversation on twitter can turn into a connection and you both follow each other.

A conversation using the @ function is like text messaging back and forth but the big difference is that your messages can be read by all your followers. When you @username another account what you sent shows up in your profile with your tweets, it is also tweeted out to your followers. If the person has messages set up to go to their cell phone then your message will go to them either through a text message or a twitter app. If the other person you messaged responds, that will show up in their tweets and all their followers will see it. Your followers will not see the response unless they click on one of the messages. If they do click on the message you sent then they will be able to see the message stream in the right hand column of their twitter page.

This messaging function is one of the greatest ways to use twitter to really connect with likeminded people. Be sure to interact daily. Like we discussed earlier including messages in with your tweets makes your account look more alive and interactive. It attracts people from both sides of the messaging to join in on the conversation.

Do not just broadcast all the time, interact. Be sure to interact with other users who have shown interest in what you have to share.

Be sure to check the @Mentions tab under your home page daily. Someone may be starting a discussion.

Twitter is not a one way street, and you need passengers along for the ride.

36. A friend of my friend

One of the best ways to find interesting people and potential followers on twitter is to look at who your friends are following and who is following them. A quick glance at these profiles may reveal likeminded people that you may want to follow. The person you follow could also see that you both follow the same people and that could spark instant camaraderie. Even a follow back could occur.

You could message them that you both follow your friend @username, and ask them a question. This could spark conversation either publicly or through a direct message.

You can search who your real life friends follow and who follows them and maybe stumble upon some one that you know personally that you had not found yet on twitter.

This is another way to find people that you want to follow who may reciprocate with a follow back.

There is a saying that an enemy of my enemy is my friend, well on twitter the friend of your friend may be a potential follower.

37. Wefollow.com

A quick and easy way to get your name out there is to register your account at wefollow.com under your interests; you can also then find others that share your interests.

It is very easy; you just go to http://wefollow.com/, in the top right hand corner you click add yourself to wefollow. You then enter the city and state you live in and five interests you have (when you enter your interests a drop down of possible choices will appear, choose the ones with the most listings by the number next to them). This will let others who visit the site know what you are interested in and could lead to more followers.

After you have entered your choice you tweet out the message at the bottom of the screen to let everyone know you just listed yourself and what your specific interests are. This could also lead to followers from people searching your tweets, we will discuss this later.

To find people with like interests you simply key in a topic at the top of the page where it says "enter a tag" then click the magnifying glass. You will then see everyone listed under that tag. Then you will have two separate tabs you can click to see either the most influential twitter user or the one with the most followers that is listed under that tag.

This is a great place to find interesting people and list yourself so potential followers can find you.

The current online information says that 350,000 people visit wefollow.com per month. This is a source of followers. Be sure to add yourself!

38. Twellow.com

Wouldn't it be great if there were yellow pages for twitter so you could list yourself and people could find you easily. Darn, what? There is?

Twellow.com the twitter yellow pages, it exists.

There are 320,000 visits to twellow.com each month and it has 30.5 million twitter profiles. This is the place you need to be listed.

You can list yourself in all the categories that you find are relevant to your topic area that you tweet about. You can find people in the specific area you may be interested in learning more about. Each category has the twitter accounts in it listed by those with the most followers and then with the 2nd most, then 3rd most followers etc. When you click categories you also get subcategories, you can get very specific with the topic area you are looking for.

To search the site, at the top of the web site you can enter categories and subcategories next to the key words like **Search:** 'football' then **Within:** 'Sports'.

For instance inside the category of football you can go to the subcategories of fantasy football, college football, NFL, or coach.

First you sign up for the site. Then you search relevant categories and click "+Add Me" to be listed in your favorite subcategories.

You have to really play around on the site and get to know how it works.

This is one of the best places to find the most popular twitter accounts that tweet about your areas of interest to follow and also to be found by people interested in your topic area.

You have to list yourself here and add yourself to all the relevant topic areas if you want to get to 1000 followers on twitter.

39. Twibes.com

With 83,000 visitors a month this site could also enable you to run into people that have the same interests.

After you authorize the twibes application you can do several different things.

Under active twibes you can find one that interests you and join it by clicking the "tweet to join" button. This will let all your followers know that you have joined the twibe. You can also click the "follow all" button to follow all the twibe members if you choose. You can invite other users to join the twibe and tweet directly to the twibe and bypass twitter altogether. This could be a pretty exclusive club.

You can search twibe topics to find a more specific twibe to join that is less active but aligns more with your specific interests. This could result in several mutual follows with likeminded people who will read your tweets because of your like mindedness.

Twibes also has twitter lists, these lists contain people who have been tagged with a topic like "social media", "real estate", or "health" etc. You can add yourself, suggest people, or invite someone to these lists. These lists are another great way to find people with like interests.

You can also be the chief of your own twibe if you are interested. You can have up to three twibes if you would like. You simply click "start twitter group", then tweet out the name of your twibe, others join by tweeting out that they joined. You can send out one public invite then tweet users directly if you really want certain people to join.

Twibes is similar to facebook groups but is limited to the 140 character tweets.

This is a great way to connect with like minded people.

A twibe may get you closer to 1000 followers.

40. Increase your opportunities

This section was all about the principle of increasing the odds that your account will be found on twitter.

Do not make the mistake of simply opening an account and tweeting great tweets with the thought that the twitterverse will discover you on its own through magic. You have to get your name out there every day and let people see you. Some of my favorite accounts to this day only have 20 to 50 followers after producing great content for months sometimes years.

If you want 1000 followers please follow the last nine tips in this section, they will do a lot to give others the chance to find you on twitter. Your twitter account is just like a good show, movie, or television show, no one will watch if they don't know about it. **You must advertise yourself on twitter.**

So do not tweet in a closed bubble.

1. Follow the top twitter accounts that are similar to your interests so people interested in that account might find you.

2. Follow accounts that you find interesting that have a lot of followers so you can interact and get more potential followers.

3. Write great tweets so when you attract viewers they will like what they see and follow you.

4. Retweet tweets from others, they might follow you.

5. Interact through messaging, to build relationships and get real followers.

6. Find people you already know by looking at your real life friend's follower lists.

7. Be sure you are listed on twitter application directory sites under all categories that apply.

Do no not be shy on twitter, be out going, communicate, interact, meet people, and get your name out there. Twitter is not for the timid it is for those who know how to promote themselves.

PART V
Where to find and get follow backs

41. Follow back or not?

On twitter there are accounts that follow back every single person that follows them. There are twitter lists, website groups, and blog pages devoted to nothing but people that follow back on twitter.

The good thing about this is that you can get hundreds and hundreds of followers in a day with little effort. The bad news is that vast majority of these people are not looking for accounts to follow they are looking for followers. There are many follow back accounts that do nothing but tweet to get followers and promo people to follow, sometimes their sole purpose on twitter is to get as many followers as is possible.

Their motivation may be to monetize their account one day by selling advertisements, or it may just be for ego, some also use their twitter to promote themselves or others in the music business. With others it is just a numbers game that is all about how many followers they can get.

Whatever the reason they are following back, they are likely no reading your tweets, which is the whole purpose of having the 1000 followers. At the same time though if someone you want to follow has the same interests as you have and they produce real tweets and have interaction with others in their tweet stream then a follow back is a bonus. If they only have 50 to 100 people that they follow it is a good chance that they will read your tweets from time to time in their tweet stream. Many of my favorite people on twitter that I have as business contacts follow back. I have one stock trading friend who has over 1200 followers and follows back all 1200. He sees my retweets and sometimes thanks me, he also comments on my tweets at times. I would follow him whether he followed me back or not, his follow back is a bonus not a requirement. I consider him a real follower, not just a reciprocal follow back. We share the same interests so people could also stumble across him in my lists of best traders on twitter and on the people I follow. Also people are recommended to follow me when I follow the same people that they do, so he is a high quality follow in addition to being a follow back, and he also reads my tweets. That is the kind of win/win/win situation you want when you are looking for follow backs.

At the same time there is a major account on twitter called @StockTwits, it is about stock trading and promoting its website. It has about 125,000 followers and it follows back. While a stock trader may follow this account because they like its content and tweets, and they get a reciprocal follow back, it is not a "real" follower. The odds are really close to zero that the people that run the @StockTwits timeline will ever read a single one of your tweets. So if you follow them and you notice they follow back do not get excited and fall under any kind of a delusion that you gained a follower and that your tweets will now be read by @StockTwits. What we are aiming at is 1000 REAL followers that want to hear what you have to say, not auto follow backs that will never even look at your tweets. So while it is good that you follow an account that shares your interests and you scored a "follower", this is not what we are aiming at, it is just a bonus.

42. Your own rules

A big question to ask yourself on twitter is will you automatically follow back every single person that follows you? Will you only follow back people that have interesting accounts and you really want to read their tweets? Will you look at each followers profile and make an individual decision each time? Will you only follow back twitter accounts that are about the same topic area? Or will you follow back everyone except people that seem a little profane or childish in their tweets?

The decision should be one that fits your personality. You may just say the more the merrier and follow back everyone. You may enjoy watching the tweet stream of hundreds of people float by on your home page. Or be very exclusive and only follow those that you will be planning to read their tweets at every chance you get.

A drawback to following everyone back is that it is hard to build connections because you are overwhelmed with followers and tweets. However this can be overcome by listing the people you follow into categories, and reading the tweet streams in different lists. A drawback to following everyone is that there are people on twitter that think the quality of your tweets is based on your follower to following ratio. If you follow 30 accounts and have 5000 following you, then you must have great tweets. At the same time there are many that do not follow accounts that do not follow back. Their opinion is that snobs do not follow back. Who do they think they are Justin Bieber? Many believe that all accounts should reciprocate by following back. Others believe that everyone should only follow accounts when they intend to read their tweets.

So we are divided between the puritans that believe in 100% authenticity in followers and following. Then we have the reciprocal follow backs that believe in a follow for a follow. Who is right and who is wrong? I say follow your personality, whatever you feel is the right thing for your account. Just don't go overboard following no one and wanting to get 1000 followers yourself. Also do not go out and follow 1000 people that you think will follow you back but have no intention of ever reading any of their tweets, I think the best course is what you feel comfortable with and do with good intentions.

43. Followback #hashtags

The hashtag sign "#" is used on twitter to mark a topic, word, or phrase and make it really easy to search. You make a word or cluster of words stand out when you place the hash mark in front of it. Searching "#followback" on twitter in the search box will give you many more quick specific results pin pointing people who follow back than searching "people who follow back". On twitter people use specific hash tags in their tweets and on their bios to identify themselves as people who always follow back. Below are the top 45 most popular hash tags on twitter that identify the account that uses it as one that will follow back anyone who follows them.

#TweepTeam
#InstantFollow
#AutoFollowBack
#IFollowBack
#InstantFollowBack
#TeamFollowBack
#teamfollow
#TF
#teamfollowback
#INST
#followme
#FollowFriday
#TAF
#GFB
#MustFollow
#FollowBack
#followall
#sougofollow
#followmejp
#AutoFollow

#Follow4Follow
#F4F
#AFB
 #500aday
 #FF
#FollowAgain
 #TFB
#100ADAY
#1000ADAY
#IFollowAll
#FollowNGain
#followdaibosyu
#followcircle
#JustFollow
#GoFollow
#FollowNow
#teamautofollowback
#TAFB
#teamautofollow
#FASTNNOW
#followbacksquad
#IFB
#FollowNow
#GoFollow
#Quickfollow
#followrapido

WARNING: Follow with caution; the majority of these accounts have no interest in what you are tweeting about, most only want followers, not someone to follow. To test this theory I created two accounts, in one I followed the principles in this book and got 40 followers in a few days, in the other I just went for follow backs and got 1500 followers in 72 hours. To see which account had what I consider "real" followers I tweeted out of both accounts for a few days. I had five times the retweets with my 40 followers than I got with the over 1500 "follow backs". While this is an unscientific test it does show the difference between the follow back circles and really finding likeminded followers. Personally I am convinced and I would not waste a lot of time chasing follow backs. All you get is a large number of followers which might make you look good to others but will produce little value for your account.

44. Twellow Follow backs

There are even more places outside of twitter itself to find follow backs if you can't help yourself.

Twellow.com is another place to go for people that have listed themselves as accounts that follow back everyone.

If you search "followback" at twellow.com you get 2,228 accounts that are listed.

A search for "autofollow" will get you an additional 213 accounts.

A search for "Ifollowback" will return 579.

It is the same principle as the hash tag, but people avoided having to waste space on their bios and sending out tweets by listing themselves here.

45. Twibes of follow backs

Not to be left out of the game, twibes.com has a twibe of 71 members that follow back. What do they talk about? There is also an auto follow twibe of 33 members.

They also have a list of 69 people who follow back.

It appears that the hash tags are far more popular than actually listing yourself under a group. If you really want, you could list yourself on one of these sites. At least you don't have to use the hash tags in tweets or your bio.

Some people on twitter actually avoid the follow back twitterverse because they believe that these people are not interested in content and adding value to a conversation, they are only follower hunting. So they avoid the whole group.

So to avoid stigma you would do much better to quietly list yourself in one of these groups than broadcast it to all your followers.

It is your choice to participate or avoid this game altogether.

Steve Burns

46. Following follow back accounts

I think the right way to follow accounts that follow back is to go look for people that share the same interests as you do. If these accounts have almost the same number of followers as those they are following, they might follow back even though they do not broadcast it.

The accounts that you will have the best luck with actually having your tweets read will be the ones that are not following a huge number of people. A great ratio and volume could be a user who is following 45, and has 45 followers, that person is likely to take the time to look at your account when you follow them. They are also likely to give you a reciprocal follow since you tweet about what they are interested in and showed interest in their account. Following an account that is following 3000 and has 3000 followers will not likely result in you acquiring a real follower they are probably already at full capacity. They may follow you back but it is unlikely that you will be someone that they really follow and read your tweets. You will need to make an effort to communicate with them if you want to get on their radar.

A great way to get your name out there is to follow accounts that tweet about the same thing you are interested in. Why not follow an account that has an equal number of followers to who they are following? If you are looking to follow some one interesting then it makes no difference if they follow 3 people and have 10,000 followers, who cares, you want to hear what they have to say. However if you are looking for followers for yourself, then it make all the difference.

To find potential followers look for an equal amount of followers versus followed, and for less than 100 accounts on both sides. This will increase your chances of getting noticed and not lost in the crowd.

Another red flag is if they are following way more accounts than are following them. If you see they are following 1000 with 150 followers this is a huge red flag that they are spammers and probably farming followers only to spam them later. If they also have zero tweets that almost makes it definite that they are spammers. Be thoughtful and careful in your pursuit of follow backs.

47. The best follow back lists

I felt like I had to include this list in the book. Some readers will salivate at the thought of gathering thousands of followers who will follow back. It is a game to some and many like the way it makes their accounts look very impressive. So here are some of the very top lists on the web that show you quickly who will follow you back. They are not 100% accurate, but over all these lists do provide a huge short cut for those gamers who want thousands and thousands of followers quickly.

WARNING: The technical follow limit is 1000 per day; put twitter has other rules prohibiting aggressive following, so proceed with caution: twitter will suspend your account if you get to aggressive.

http://www.lovejordan.net/ArticlesTop500TwitterUsers.html/

http://www.graphicsms.com/blog/863-100-top-twitter-followback-lists/

http://www.sebastienpage.com/2009/03/23/1001-twitter-users-follow-back/

http://socialnewswatch.com/top-twitter-users/

http://atniz.com/2010/03/02/biggest-twitter-follow-back-list/

http://assetebooks.com/social-media/top-10-twitter-follow-back-lists

48. Will they follow back?

As you go in pursuit of followers who you think will follow you back you do need to be mindful of a few things. If they have not tweeted since 2008 it is a good sign that the account was abandoned long ago. Regardless of if you see #followback or they are on a list of follow backs that does not guarantee they will follow back. Many people set up accounts and then get sick of them and move on. If all they were doing was gaming for follow backs then I do not blame them for getting sick of the game and quitting. This is not a good use of twitter as a sole purpose for your account.

Also if they are listed on a site as a follow back but follow 200 people but have 1000 followers then they are not following back regardless of what they say. A true follow back should have equal or slightly more accounts they are following versus followers. This discrepancy could also mean that they abandoned the account long ago but people kept piling in to follow hoping for a follow back but never got one, and they did not bother to find out and unfollow the account.

Also if the account you are expecting a follow back from is following over 2000 accounts but has less than 1820 followers then they very likely cannot follow back anyone if they wanted. As of this writing according to many websites and based on my own personal experience you can follow up to about 2002 accounts then 10% more accounts than those that follow you after that. If you have 2000 followers then you can follow 2200 accounts, if you have 10,000 followers you can follow 11,000 accounts.

So if you decide to go grab 1000 follow backs to make your account look like it is hopping with activity just be sure not to follow any ghosts of twitter past. You want to follow active accounts that will at least follow you back, even though they will probably never read a single tweet from you.

49. Don't overdo it

Remember easy does it with the follow backs if that is something you decide to pursue. The only value I can see is if you are new to twitter and have zero followers, getting a few hundred quick follow backs from the biggest follow back account could help get your name out there and look like a big shot. I would use this tactically and follow back only the top one hundred or so accounts that have 100,000+ or 50,000+ followers that will get you on the radar of the thousands of people that also follow those same people. Unfortunately they will probably be people that are interested only in follow backs not reading tweets.

Follow backs can get quickly out of hand and take away from your quality time on twitter that needs to be spent sending out great tweets and interacting with real people with common interests.

You can follow a certain person then get flooded with followers that are all expecting a follow back. Once again do not get too excited these people are not mobbing you to connect, just to score a follower themselves.

If you go out and follow one thousand people on the first day you will turn off real followers who see the following 1000 versus followers 23 on your profile, they will think you are a spammer and stay away. Just pursue maybe a hundred of the top follow backs with a ton of followers and leave it at that. Or do it in 50 to 100 a day to get you to the number you want, then get serious about finding real followers.

Do not let your pursuit of automatic follow backs cause you to lose REAL followers.

50. Unfollow with ease

What the heck? I followed 500 accounts that were supposed to follow back but five days later only have 300 followers?

Some accounts don't follow back immediately, some take up to a week. Whenever you are tired of waiting, how do you find out and unfollow the uncooperative people who were suppose to follow back? What do you do if they played you? They followed you, you automatically followed them back and then they stopped following you and went looking for more suckers.

Do you go unfollow everyone you are following and then follow back only the accounts that are following you? Only if you want to risk getting your account suspended for what is called follower churn at twitter. That is frowned upon.

The easiest way I have found that really lets you look at each account before you unfollow and really pick and choose who to unfollow is the site manageflitter.com. Here is the url: http://manageflitter.com/content/who-unfollowed-me-on-twitter

It is very easy to use.

You click: **Start using manage twitter**

Then: **Connect to twitter**

You will see: **Not following back on the left**

You will see page numbers at the top; you will need to click on each page to see all the accounts that are not following you. Click the boxes next to accounts that you want to unfollow. Be careful not to unfollow your favorites.

When you are done with your selections click: **Unfollow '#' selected.**

Now you have stop following the accounts that did not reciprocate.

Even if you are not pursuing follow backs and only following back your followers you will be surprised at how many people follow you, and then unfollow. Most of them are just trying to get noticed by as many accounts as possible. They want to get their tweets in your tweet stream then move on to other victims. Do not let this happen to you. Twitter is "bird eat bird" out there, be careful.

PART VI
Interacting on twitter

51. Use direct messages for privacy

If someone is following you then you can send them a direct message. If there is something that you want to tell them privately then don't hesitate. Interacting builds relationships on twitter, and that is what it is all about.

I direct message other authors to ask them if they would be willing to write a blurb for my book. By doing this privately instead of publicly they can say no. I am not putting them "on the spot" with a public tweet. That would just be rude.

I have also used a private direct message to exchange phone numbers or email addresses. You probably don't want your 1000 real followers to have your personal phone number. Many of the money managers I tweet with do not want to give out their personal e-mails to the general public.

You can ask them questions that are not appropriate for a tweet stream. I think of direct messaging on twitter being like a baby email with 140 characters.

Use the messages to build stronger relationships and network, not to spam.

Do not send affiliate links, or your product links as a direct message. That puts you on the spam list of real twitter users and could cause people to stop following you very quickly.

Be sure to read all your messages daily, either on twitter directly under the message tab or set them up to come to your e-mail if that is what you always check. Be sure to watch your messages daily, you never know what kind of opportunity could pop up. It would be a shame if you got a break in your field but didn't look at your messages and missed it all together, or you stumbled on the message a week later but the opportunity had passed. Read them all daily.

So use direct messages to connect and build relationships. It is a great tool.

52. Always respond to DMs that are real

If you get a direct message then always respond. If it is simply a complement then say thank you. If it is a conversation then keep the messages going back and forth. Share things about yourself and ask the other person what they are interested in and for their opinions. Share information, ask questions, have a conversation.

Now if you get direct messages with links that are obviously spam and the sender gets paid per click, or is trying to sell a product then you do not need to respond. Unless it is to say "stop spamming me".

Real direct messages are a chance to connect. Do not miss the chance. With the flood of tweets and message spam on twitter the sender will not even know for sure if you read it unless you respond in some way.

So just like tweets, people like to know someone is reading their messages. Let them know by responding.

53. Check and respond to @communications

Just like with direct messages, you do not want to miss a chance to interact when someone sends you a direct tweet. By putting the '@' in front of your username a tweet has an active link to your account in it. If you have your cell phone set up for direct tweets then you will receive these through a text message or on your twitter application.

If it is a public message to you, then you need to respond back to show the sender you are active on twitter. Many times like I have said before, these public messages evolve into a full blown conversation with facts, opinions, and thoughts. Your followers will be able to see your response tweets or the whole conversation by clicking on one the tweets. At times other followers on either side of the conversation will join in and list both of you in their tweets so you both see the tweet conversation continuing. This is a great way to build those connections I keep talking about.

Also you might get am @message because you have been included in a list on a tweet.

#FollowFriday @SJosephBurns @Dowbuys @DanZanger @DarvasTrader

This is example of a tweet that I might tweet out on Friday for suggestions on people for other stock traders to follow on twitter. All these people will get the @message that I tweeted. If you are in a list like this be sure to reciprocate in some way. Either with a thanks tweet, a retweet, or a #FollowFriday that includes them this week or next week. This is a great comple-ment, appreciate them for doing it.

You may also get a message through a retweet.

RT @SJosephBurns "Simplicity is the key to brilliance". –Bruce Lee

This is a copied retweet with an RT just added to your tweet. If you just push the retweet button on the tweet of another person it just sends out the tweet exactly the way you sent it. When it is done this way then you see it as a @message instead of under the retweet tab on your home page. So this is just like a retweet. Be sure to show your appreciation in some way. This gets your name out in front of all the followers of the person who retweeted you, it could result in more real followers if it is a great tweet and it is tweeted out at a time where it will be read and not lost in a lot of other tweets.

Be sure to check the @mentions tab on your home page for any public tweets addressed to you that you may have missed.

54. Always thank retweets

Rules #1 always check your retweet tab daily.

Rule #2 always thank the retweeter in some way.

Rule #3 never forget rules numbers 1 and 2.

Do not miss a chance to interact with appreciation for a retweet. These are very valuable in the Twitterverse because it shows that someone really liked your tweet so much that they decided to share it with all their followers. This gets your name in front of all of the accounts followers and may result in you picking up a few real followers to get you closer to the 1000 goal.

You can thank the retweeter in a few different ways.

1. You can retweet one of their best tweets to your followers.

2. You can thank them with a @message publicly.

3. You can thank them in a direct private message.

4. You can recommend them on follow Friday.

5. You can send them a message saying you like the information they tweet.

6. You can follow them back if you are not already following them.

7. You can put them on a list for their topic area or a My Retweeters list.

Whether they push the retweet button on your tweet and send it out as is, or use the RT letter option with your @username, be sure you are aware of the gesture and reciprocate in some way.

You get more of what you recognize and appreciate.

55. Follow Friday shout outs

What exactly is a follow Friday?

The idea is to think of interesting people you already follow and recommend them to others. People mainly use the #FollowFriday hashtag to send out their own recommendations and also to locate recommendations from other twitter accounts. The #FollowFriday hash tag will be seen by all the followers of the person who sends the tweet even if it is not found in search by others. This will also send the accounts listed a direct tweet because your @username will be on the tweet.

Being on a #FollowFriday tweet can lead to your account picking up 10 to 20 or more real followers. It depends on how many followers the person has that recommends you.

How do you get on a follow Friday tweet?

You send out great tweets, you inform, entertain, and make followers feel like you can teach them about a given topic. They have to want to share your account with others. If they love your tweets then you could make the list. So think about your tweets and make them great, avoid getting sloppy or lazy and lowering your quality.

Also participate in follow Friday, share your favorite four or five accounts each Friday. The accounts you really like reading and that add value to your experience on twitter. You may get the accounts attention and a thank you. Or better yet they may reciprocate by recommending you that day or the next Friday.

Another great thing is when your follow Friday tweet is retweeted by one of the people you recommended and your name is added. That can score several new followers.

So make it part of your weekly routine to participate in follow Friday and help get others names out there, it is good karma, and you reap what you sow.

56. Use your cell phone to tweet

Just because you are away from your desk top, lap top, or iPad doesn't mean you have to be away from the twitterverse.

Today almost everyone has a smart phone that they can download a twitter app and stay connected. Any cell phone with text messaging can be set up to receive tweets from specific accounts, receive @messages, or direct messages, and tweet by using the phone number 40404 in the United States. (Check twitter for the number in your country if you live outside the U.S.)

To adjust what kind of tweets you will receive through your phone go to the picture of your profile on the top right corner and click settings, then mobile, you will see:

Text message notifications

• ☑   Tweets from people you've enabled for mobile notifications

   • ☑   Direct messages

   • ☑   Mentions and replies

      o ⊙ Only from people I follow

      o ☐ From anyone

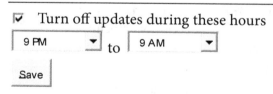

You can set these to your preferences. You do not want to miss an important tweet while you are out, but you also do not want a tweet at 2 a.m. in the morning. Stay connected if you are truly serious about getting to 1000 followers, it will only take a second to respond to a message.

57. Hash tags put you in the flow

When you send a tweet your followers see it, and people who search for specific words contained in your tweet see it. Then it may die and go to tweet heaven and never be seen again by anyone. Amen, may it rest in peace.

However if you tweet about a stock trade and end your tweet with #stocks or #stockmarket then people searching for that topic by using your specific hash tag will see it in their stream when they search for it. Your followers may find it then maybe others. If they find your tweet interesting you may score a retweet and then any of the new followers of that account that see it may retweet it. That is how tweets go viral.

It would help spread your tweets around and give them more visibility by adding hash tags to the majority of your tweets that fall into a specific category. Some people are interested in things like inspirational quotes. So they will simply search "#quotes" and get their fill of quotes for the day. **If your quotes are not hash tagged then your tweets will simply drift away invisible to this eager searcher.**

Here are some of the most popular hash tags on twitter organized by topic.

Business: #jobs, #business, #networking, #retail, #shoppers, #consumer, #sales, #economy, #technology, #luxury, #news, #internet, #mktg, #marketing, #webmarketing

Celebrities: #50cent, #aplusk, #bieber, #britneyspears, #charliesheen, #ladygaga, #obama, #oprah, #osama, #perezhilton, #ryanseacrest, #the_real_shaq, #theellenshow

Education: #edapp, #edtech, #education, #elearning, #lrnchat, #mlearning, #teachers

Environment / Justice: #humanrights, #poverty, #hunger, #aid, #sustainability, #health, #green, #eco, #earthtweet, #humantrafficking, #climate, #solar, #fairtrade

Social Change: #socialgood, #cause, #volunteer, #4change, #giveback, #dogood, #crisiscommons

TV Entertainment: #bones, #dwts, #glee, #gossipgirl, #graysanatomy, #idol, #lrnchat, #mlearning, #sharktank, #survivor, #teachers, #theoffice, #thevoice, #xfactor

These are some suggestions, but keep your eyes open for interesting hash tags used by popular people that are on your topic area. Search them and see if they are popular if they are you need to use them on tweets that apply to your topic area of choice.

If I tweet out a quote by itself only a few people see it that happen to be watching at that time. If I add a hash tag it can be seen through searches by many more people for a much longer period of time. Give your tweet wings; use the correct hash tags to optimize twitter searches for it.

58. Use the '$' for talking stocks

If you will never, ever, tweet a stock symbol or be interested in any stock then skip this tip. However if you have any interest in stocks, investing, or trading then this is a symbol you need to know about.

@Stocktwits claims to have invented using the '$' symbol before a stock symbol to tag in on twitter. So the stock of Citigroup goes from just a 'C' to '$C', General Motors stock goes from 'GM' to '$GM' and so on. This is like a hash tag just a different symbol is used to create a different tag to search for.

If you want to search people talking about Citigroup's stock then '$C' will take you to it directly. Searching the word Citigroup will likely lead to people discussing news or opinions about the company as a whole and a search of 'C' will lead to people using it as the word 'see' so the '$' is simple in its brilliance and makes it possible for stock traders and investors to see what people are saying about a given stock at any time of day.

If you are a stock trader that trades only a few stocks primarily at any given time what would be a better way to find like-minded people than by locating who is talking about the same stock you are trading? Search the '$stocksymbol' for the company you are interested in. Do not be shy, start a conversation through public tweeting. Ask about their opinions. Find out why they believe what they do about the future of the company. Why do they think the stock will go up or down? This is a great tool to see what others opinions are and if they see something you do not in fundamental valuation, or price action. You might even decide to follow them because of their knowledge or gain a follower because they want to learn from you.

So if you are tweeting about stocks always use the '$' sign in front of the ticker symbol so you turn the random letters that will be lost in the ocean of tweets into a searchable symbol for people that want to hear what is being said about that stock currently on twitter.

59. Twitter language shorthand

On twitter tweets are in English most of the time, but sometimes they are also in other languages. Tweets come out in all languages, Spanish, French, Japanese, and sometimes Twitterish.

The tweet:

> "We will see if General Motors stock rallies tomorrow to a new high, what do you think and why?"

In Twitterish it would be:

> "We'll c if $GM rallies tomorrow 2 a new hi, what do u think & why? #stocks"

In an effort to get as much information into one tweet as possible, twitter users sometimes use letters and symbols to signify words. There is an art to using enough shorthand to shorten the amount of characters without using too much and causing the reader to not understand the tweet.

While many of the shorthand ideas are obvious, the following list are a few of the most popular sayings abbreviated into clusters of letters.

OH = Overheard. 'OH' is commonly used at conferences or while traveling. OH indicates a quotation of someone else's remarks.

DM = Direct Message. DMs are Twitter's email. "DM me" means take the discussion private

@= At. The symbol @ can be used to express 'at,' as in location in addition to a direct tweet to a twitter username used after the symbol. Use a space to prevent a direct tweet to the account of the same name.

BTW = By The Way. BTW is an easy way to add an aside.

FTW = For The Win. Whatever the action or product FTW modifies is *good*.

FTL = For The Loss (or For The Lose). FTL is generally an expression of disappointment, disapproval or dismay. It's the opposite of FTW

IRL = In Real Life. What's true on Twitter may not be true IRL.

FTF = Face to Face. FTF or F2F refers to an actual meeting in person, IRL. That can mean at a tweetup or other occasion where you might encounter other Twitterers.

IMHO = In My Honest Opinion. IMHO usually indicates that 'This is an op-ed tweet, not a factual assertion.' UPDATE: It can be argued that "Humble" is the more common meaning, but both are valid for IMHO

YMMV = Your Mileage May Vary. In other words (IOW), what's true in my experience (IMX) may differ from yours if you try _____ product/service/technique.

BR = Best Regards. BR is a useful way of being cordial, particularly when making a difficult request, submitting a complaint, or when introducing yourself.

b/c = because. b/c is not the same as the blind carbon copy (BCC) used in email.

JV = Joint Venture. A JV refers to a collaborative enterprise between Twitterers on a project.

LMK = Let Me Know. Tweet me back (TMB) when you have more information about a question or a decision on a request.

NSFW = Not Safe For Work warns you of inappropriate links that should not be clicked on a workplace computer.

LMAO = Laughing My A** Off. This comes up a fair bit, no doubt because there is plenty to laugh about on Twitter and in the wide world.

LOL=Laughing out Loud. This is very popular and almost everyone knows it. Use these abbreviations to shorten your tweets but do not overdo it to the point that your followers will not understand the tweet.

60. Feed to facebook

Do you want to instantly gain a lot of new followers who are likely to read your tweets? Then connect your twitter account to your facebook account. Then your facebook friends become your twitter followers automatically. Your tweets start feeding into your facebook account and post on your wall.

There are a few ways you can choose to do this. The two most common ways are listed below.

You can use the simple facebook application for twitter at the following url.

http://www.facebook.com/apps/application. php?id=2231777543

Or use the twitter application for facebook at the following url.

http://twitter.com/about/resources/widgets/facebook

Just follow the step by step instructions if you decide to link the two.

WARNING: If you use twitter and facebook very differently from each other then you may not want to link the two. If facebook is primarily for family and friends and you use twitter for specialized information and affiliate links then they may not mesh together and you may lose some facebook friends.

If you send out an excessive amount of tweets a day, this may be fine on twitter because many are never seen unless it is at peak times. But on facebook you may annoy your friends or family who are interested in your real life updates.

However if you have a large amount of facebook friends and business associates for networking, and you only send out high quality tweets a few times a day. Then linking the two could extend the reach of your tweets and you could end up with facebook friends 'liking' your tweets which will show up as a like on their facebook wall, sort of like a retweet. Done correctly, this will extend the reach of your tweets and may also cause several of your facebook friends that are on twitter to become a real follower on twitter, this has been the case for me.

So just remember to not over due your tweets if it includes your facebook friends and family. Also remember who your audience is.

PART VII
Broadcast your twitter account

61. Facebook

Some people will choose not to feed their tweets into facebook because they use them differently. For me facebook is for building relationships by letting your facebook friends know what you are about. Twitter to me is more like a quick way to share information with people that have the same interests. You could have 50,000 real followers on twitter with no problem but facebook is built to have 5000 facebook friends maximum, and at some point it is hard to really be "friends" with that many people. However there is no limit to how many followers you can have without losing the value of the information shared.

What I do is give my facebook friends updates when I reach certain thresholds on twitter. I share the link to my twitter account and post a status update like "I now have 4000 followers on twitter". I share how I like the service and how I use it. I have gained many followers on twitter by my facebook friends seeing that and following me; I always follow my facebook friends back and list them on a friends list on twitter.

Your facebook profile has a place where you can list your twitter screen name. You can list your twitter address under info>contact information>edit>screen name. Under IM screen names you enter your '@username' then in the drop down box you select 'twitter'. After you save the changes this creates a live link from your facebook info page to your twitter account. People can easily find you on twitter if they find you on facebook if your profile is open to the public. I believe many people found me this way. When people do not feel comfortable sending you a friend request because it may be too personal for them, they can follow you on twitter. You have given them a second option.

If you have a facebook fan page for your business or product don't forget to list you twitter account there also under info>general information.

Do not miss out on this opportunity; enter your twitter account under your contact information on facebook. If you do not have a facebook profile page then you need to join the world in the 21st century and set one up. It is just a modern form of communication, do not be afraid.

62. Amazon.com

If you do not write any reviews for products on Amazon then you can skip this idea. If you have written many reviews for a specific kind of item or you are a top reviewer this could be a gold mine.

Simply list your twitter user name on your Amazon profile page in the section labeled "In my own words". I simply put "follow me on twitter>@SJosephBurns".

I am a top reviewer on Amazon and get from 150 to 200 views of my profile page a month. This is a lot of potential followers. It works perfectly for me because I write reviews about trading books and inspirational books, and I tweet about stock trading, inspirational quotes, and books. So if people love the information I share in my reviews they can get more of the same by following me on twitter. I also tweet out every one of my new reviews from Amazon whether the review says the item is good or bad. Followers find both kinds of reviews to be helpful in their buying decisions.

Twitter has been a natural extension of my Amazon profile. I now share opinions and information in 140 characters or less when using my twitter account for the same purpose as my Amazon reviews. It has really been fun trying to write a one sentence review while tweeting out the link to my full Amazon review. My followers have given positive feedback for doing this.

So if you are an avid Amazon reviewer in a specific area of products that tie into your twitter account be sure to list your twitter username so your Amazon followers can become your twitter followers.

63. E-mail signature line

How many of us have an automatic signature line on our business or home e-mail? You know the one you set up so you do not have to key in your name on every e-mail you send? What if you tweet about the business you are in? Would it make sense to put your twitter user name on your e-mail so that all your work associates see it?

Steve Burns
Author/Trader
twitter @SJosephBurns

It does if you are in a specific business and tweet about that industry. It may not make sense if you tweet about yourself and minutia in your daily life.

It would make sense if you are an author and you e-mail other writers, publishers, and fans.

Twitter is another form of communication and I think it ties in well with e-mail; some of the people you e-mail may be very interested in what you have to say on a daily basis, especially if you are a top professional, manager, or leader in your field of expertise.

I have done this and picked up some followers through simple communicating that I was on twitter on the bottom of an e-mail.

If you decide this does make sense to you, just be sure to remember who your audience is and always keep it professional if you have business colleagues following you.

Do not tweet out anything that would embarrass you if it was on the front page of the newspaper.

64. Business card

If you still hand out business cards then your twitter user-name needs to be on it.

Steve Burns
Author/Trader/Book Reviewer/Blogger
Email: stephenburns@bellsouth.net
twitter@SJosephBurns
615-555-5555

Just like with e-mail this works best when you tweet about the topics your potential business associates would be interested in. What a great way to merge the timeless business card with a modern form of communication like twitter.

In the future twitter, facebook, and LinkedIn may be more important than e-mail. For now your twitter username is an easy way for someone to find you on the site and follow you and see your work and what you are about. Potentially more high value followers and that is what we are looking for.

65. MySpace

If you are still on MySpace because that is where your friends are at, and never moved over to facebook, then that is where you need to let everyone know you are now on twitter.

Many people that got into MySpace built huge networks of friends and it would be the place for them to promote their new twitter address.

Even if you have left MySpace for facebook, LinkedIn, or twitter your old friends my still be active, you should be able to go back into your account and still let everyone know that you are active at a new site. You may even cause some of your old friends on MySpace to be your new followers on twitter. You may even be their twitter mentor. (Just remember if they want to know how to get 1000 followers on twitter to go buy this book).

66. LinkedIn

If you are on LinkedIn did you already fill out your profile to include your twitter username?

All you have to do is go under Edit Profile and edit your username right by the line designated as 'twitter' that is pretty straight forward.

If you are an active user of LinkedIn this will give all your business associates your twitter username. This of course is ideal if you tweet about the business you are in. For example, if you are a motivational speaker and tweet motivational and inspirational tweets then it ties together perfectly. If people learn what you are all about from your extensive LinkedIn profile and are interested in learning more about you and the business you are in, then this could gain you a real follower. This is the ideal place where someone who is truly interested in what you have to say on a professional level can find you.

Don't miss out on this opportunity; it is one of the best places on the web to list your twitter account so people can find it.

67. At work

Do you talk about more than just work when you are at work? Could lunch breaks and coffee breaks be a chance to discuss twitter at work? If this is possible where you work it may turn your coworkers into your twitter followers. If you share common interests about sports and you tweet about sports it makes sense. How do you know if your co-workers and friends at work have a twitter account if you don't ask?

I have made some really great contacts in the work place, even through vendors and customers (if that is appropriate where you work). You may not share a common interest except twitter, and that could be enough. I have created meaningful twitter connections this way in the past. It has lead to several followers, and a lot of communication and sharing of ideas about the use of twitter itself. This has also lead to secondary followers through shout outs from my new twitter friends and their recommendations to follow me if they were interested in the stock market.

This example is not a theory it worked for me and can work for you. Just remember to use good judgment and only discuss twitter when it is allowed and appropriate at your place of business. It could lead to twitter followers and connections you never even thought of that were right under your nose.

68. Text it out

If you are one of those people that love to text up a storm then twitter was made for you. Especially if through the day you love to send your friends texts about your random thoughts, feelings, and observations. I know I am one of these people. I loved to send out texts to my friends and spouse that I thought were funny or just sharing a thought of the day. Twitter allowed me to send these 'texts' out to thousands of people. What great fun. I went from a text to five friends to over 5,000 followers. Now instead of just a "LOL" back or a "that's the truth" now I can get a retweet or a comment. I enjoy sending the tweet because it allows me to express myself, then I get to see who agrees.

What you can do to get followers is to turn your texting buddies into your followers on twitter with you following back. You could create a list of "My texting buddies" and follow each other throughout the day. This can be done on any smart phone or you can set up their specific tweets to come directly to your phone. So you are using the same principles only with a broader audience and you are making your tweets public, unless you opt to only show your tweets to your followers, but what is the point of private tweets? Isn't the whole point to get followers and get your name, product, and thoughts out there?

Converting texting to tweeting is a very simple act of using 40404 (in the U.S.) instead of your buddies' cell phone numbers. If this sounds like another cool way for you to get followers then get this method a try. All you have to do is send a text to your buddies saying you are on twitter and your username, and ask them to sign up if they have not already.

69. Are you an author?

As I was finishing my second book to be published "New Trader, Rich Trader: How to Make Money in the Stock Market" I had an idea. Why not put my twitter username in the back along with my e-mail? So that is what I did. At the end of the book I gave readers multiple ways to connect with me if they were interested.

Contact Steve:
E-Mail: stephenburns@bellsouth.net
Facebook: https://www.facebook.com/SteveJBurns
Twitter: @SJosephBurns

That definitely got my twitter username in front of readers who truly might have an interest in following me and seeing what else I had to say if they liked my book. I do not know how many followers this lead to or will help me to gain in the future, but I do know that I have several hundred very engaged followers that actively read my tweets, retweet me, and click my links at all times of the day and night. Some of them may have been the readers of my book and found me on twitter by the contact information.

The great thing is that the book is a free advertisement and will be there not only for as long as the book is in print but if the book goes out of print the remaining books can still float around for years and decades.

My first book "How I Made Money Using the Nicolas Darvas System" sold over hundreds and hundreds of copies in less than a year, if my second book does that well or better that is several hundred potential twitter followers. Not only is it a great way to advertise my account in front of hundreds and maybe thousands of followers but it is perfectly targeting the people that may want to follow me, that are interested in my topic area and may get the most value out of my tweets. So if you are a writer and the author of a book, book review, magazine or newspaper article be sure to include your twitter username at the end of your work.

70. Where are you active online?

Do not forget to let people know that you are on twitter wherever you are most active and interact with many people. If that is YouTube, and you have a popular channel or account then you may mention your twitter username at the end of your video or show it on the screen. You may want to list in on your YouTube profile.

Wherever you are most popular, it may be a site I do not even know about yet. It could be a specialized social network, or a blog, or your website. You want to use all these different locations to promote your twitter account. You just have to have a simple "follow me on twitter" with a link to click through to your account.

If you have a sports blog with one hundred followers and you have planned to tweet about sports then it may be possible to convert many of your blog followers to twitter followers. If they love your blog articles they should also be interested in your micro-blog tweets. Your blog could be the meal and your tweets could be like snacks.

If one thousand people visit your mixed martial arts website each month then they may want to follow you on twitter to get updates about the sport and even use your twitter tweets to update them with links to new articles posted on your site. Your website could gain you real followers, and then your twitter account could drive traffic to your website. That is the perfect marriage of social media.

Where do you spend the most time online? Do the people you interact with know you are on twitter and what your username is?

Do you have a blog? Do you have an available link to click to enable people to follow you?

Do you have a website? Does your site have a link to your twitter account?

PART VIII
Find likeminded people

71. Did you invite your friends?

Do you have a lot of contacts in your e-mail? Twitter allows you to invite a single person or all your contacts to join and connect through twitter.

You go to the twitter main page, you click "who to follow" then you click the tab down lower called "find friends". You can then choose the e-mails of Yahoo!, G-mail, AOL, Hotmail, and Windows Live Messenger. You will choose the e-mail that you use and click "Search Contacts". When the search box pops up you will need to click "agree", or "grant access" etc. whatever appears for that user. This will allow you to follow all the accounts of people that already are on twitter and signed up using the e-mail account that is in your contacts. You will probably want to follow them, they may give you a reciprocal follow since they know you, and this may be a source of a friend on twitter and be great for direct tweets back and forth. You will also be able to click the option that tells you how many e-mail contacts are not currently on twitter and invite them. This option sends an e-mail with a link as a quick way to join the twittersphere. If they decide to sign up then there is a very good chance that they will follow you and learn what twitter is all about.

This is how facebook and twitter grew to be so big, viral e-mails that were sent to friends then friends of friends, and caused it to grow and grow. If you have a close network of friends, family, colleagues, or fans that you are in close contact on email then this could lead to you picking up several new followers that never took the time to sign up for twitter but may do so just to communicate with you. Do not leave this out of your ideas to connect with people.

72. Monitter

Searching on twitter confusing and frustrating? Are you not finding exactly what you are looking for? How would you like to have a top notch search engine for twitter? It is at http://www.monitter.com/. Monitter allows you to search in real time any key words. This allows you to see who is tweeting about you, your interests, or a current event, etc. This can give you leads for people to connect with. You can join conversations with likeminded people talking about things that are of interest. You can also easily find people that are talking about your business or products if that is what you are looking for.

Before you are able to search you will have to go to http://www.monitter.com/ and click "connect to twitter", then "connect" to give the application access to your account.

For example I can go on monitter and search the title of my second book. I go to the web site and key in "New Trader, Rich Trader" at the top of the site next to the words "tweets containing". Then I just push "enter" on my computer key pad. On this particular day I see fourteen people that tweeted out a recent book review. I go to each of their usernames and click them. Then I will click the "view complete profile on twitter" if the profile looks interesting and they tweet about the stock market and trading I will follow them to let them know I am on twitter. They are like a lead, they showed interest in my book so they may have interest in my twitter account and I may find them interesting and follow them. This is how I use monitter to specifically find people who could likely be real followers.

You can use the above as an example, but you will have to think of specific groups of words to search that will lead you to potential followers, mutual follows, and likeminded people that are your target audience. It may be as simple as people who tweeted out an article from your blog or website. Or the same link to an article that you loved that is about your tweet topic.

73. Who is following who?

In my stock trading my main mentor through books was the legendary Nicolas Darvas. In fact my success in trading the Darvas System in the stock market was what led to my first published book. I read his books over and over and his style really fit my aggressive personality and desire to make money. So, how great was it when I found a twitter account called @DarvasTrader? This was one account that I really enjoyed reading each tweet; we were on the same page. It was sometimes odd that he would tweet out what I was thinking the market was telling me through price and volume action. Many of his followers also subscribed to his excellent newsletter Darvas Trader Pro. He had great interaction with his followers and they avidly read his tweets.

If my primary interest was the Darvas Trading System and I tweeted about the principles used by Nicolas Darvas where would people be that were also interested? Following @DarvasTrader, seemed like a logical place. So for them to find out about me I had to follow them. Of course some of them were randomly following that account and had no interest in Darvas so they would not even care about my tweet topic, but others would see on my bio that I was the author of the book "How I made Money Using the Nicolas Darvas System" and would be interested and follow me back. Following his followers was a way for me to let people with the same interests as I had know that I was tweeting about the same thing. Do not make the mistake on twitter of just tweeting and waiting for people to find you, go out and follow people that have the same interests, you want them to know you exist. If they never show any interest in you or your tweets, or the account is just inactive, then you can always unfollow them and move on. Most twitter accounts at least read the bio of the people that are following them so you will at least put your account in front of them so they can make a decision to be interested or not. This might give you a 50/50 chance of gaining a follower while not following them gives you an almost 100% chance that they will never know your account exists.

Some of the followers you are looking for are probably following your favorite twitter account if their tweets are on the same topic as yours are. You can look for evidence on the person's bio to see if they list the interests you are tweeting about, this is a double check before you follow them. This could be tricky because many people list incomplete profiles and may have varied interests.

People that may want to follow you may currently be following your favorites, so go find them and establish the first follow, most people look at the bio of all their followers to see if they want to follow back. Give them that opportunity.

74. Follow twiends

Twiends.com is very simple and easy to sign up for; you must also authorize the application to connect with your twitter account. After signing up and connecting with twitter you will be able to list yourself by entering your interests and also have access to finding people with the same interests to follow, and hopefully get some follow backs that are interested in your tweets.

The website allows you to receive "seeds" depending on who you follow. You can also buy seeds so you can advertise yourself and offer seeds for follows. There are services on the site that you can receive by buying "seeds", click the "Seeds, purchase reports" tab for more details.

Clicking "New" and then "same interests" will give you other accounts that share the same interests as you do. People are called "tweeps" on twiends.com. Putting your cursor over the twitter profile on the site will give you a pop up box showing their bio, last tweet, when they joined twitter, and the link on their profile page. You can follow accounts that you find that match your own twitter account topic and connect.

By clicking the "All" tab at the top of the website you will see accounts listed under the topics that you listed as your interests when you registered for twiends. You then click your interest name above the profile groupings and you will be able to follow people right there from the twiends website who have listed themselves as interested in that topic. Here is another great place to connect with likeminded people. This is much easier than searching twitter looking for clues of possible matches, they have listed their interest for you, and they want to connect.

This is an excellent source for matching people with like interests quickly and easily. Take advantage of it.

75. Follow your facebook friends

In the name of leaving no stone unturned in our quest for 1000 followers, our next step is to actually see if we have any of our facebook friends who missed our status updates about our twitter account and are not following us. Some of our casual acquaintances will have also been missed as we searched our e-mail contact list if we have never e-mailed them or put them as a contact.

So on our own profile page we simply click on each of the profiles of our friends one at a time and click their "info" on the left side of their profile and page down to the section that says "screen name" and look for a twitter @username with a "(twitter)" beside it. If we find this all we have to do is click the @username and it will take us to the friends twitter profile and we simply click "follow".

This is another excellent way to find people that will be interested in following you, because you are already friends. I keep a closer eye on the tweets of my facebook friends than just about any group of people. You may want to create a list for them entitled "facebook friends". Whatever you choose to do, these are people that you need to connect with on twitter if you have not already.

76. Follow your LinkedIn connections

Some people are massively involved with LinkedIn. This is the place many people go to connect and network for business purposes even if they do not have a facebook account. As of this writing, LinkedIn.com is currently ranked as the #207th most popular website in the world. This is a place you really need to take advantage of to connect with people that will likely be interested in connecting with you. If you have been active on LinkedIn and have numerous connections from your work or business this could be a gold mine. You are always much more likely to get a reciprocal follow back from people interested in business and networking. They may not have thought about following each other on twitter, but you have, thanks to reading this book.

Here are the directions to look for a twitter account on each of your connections profiles and follow them. (These instructions will give you a shot at connecting on twitter with people you already know only if they have listed a twitter account on their profile. However you won't know unless you look.)

After signing in to LinkedIn.com>click contacts>my connections>click the box with the profile>click the person's name>click on their username next to twitter on their profile>follow.

This process will, like the other 99 ideas listed in this book move you closer to 1000 real followers.

77. Follow people that list you

If you want to really build a network and connect with likeminded people, I would suggest staying very aware of who is listing you. How many times you are listed is right next to how many followers you have on your profile page. If you are listed under a complimentary list like "Best Stock Traders on twitter" then I would click the list and then click to the profile of the creator of the list. If you are not following this person I would do so. I personally always make sure I am following anyone on twitter that adds value to my account even if they do not follow back. This will also link you into their network and people that check out who is following them, so it could lead to more followers if your tweet topics are closely connected and they have loyal followers.

Most importantly though you should connect with someone who took the time to really list you so that you retain their interest and you do not lose them as a follower in the future. You want to follow back to build goodwill. When you do read their tweets and tweet out the really good ones that will be appreciated especially if you have hundreds or thousands of followers.

Also if you are on a complimentary list of a very popular and well respected twitter user in your topic area then making this list may cause people to follow you.

On the other hand if you are listed on some auto list that simply is called "People I recently followed" or "People who recently followed me" and/or has the message "A self-updating list of people who I recently followed me (generated by @formulists) then there is no need to take action. This is obviously an automatically generated list and the person has no interest in you or your tweets. They probably also sent you a message when you followed them with a link to sell you something even though you do not know them at all.

Being truly listed is a compliment, always show goodwill to the person that listed you. If you have a strict rule to only follow the people if you read their tweets daily then at least list them back. Always take opportunities to connect with people that show an interest in you. You can't get to 1000 real followers if you do not interact.

78. Follow your retweeters

I believe that on twitter people that retweet you are the best followers. Most of the people that have retweeted me have done so numerous times, they have asked me direct questions when I send out certain tweets, and have congratulated me on personal successes. These are your real followers, your continual retweeters. Even if you do have a very strict follow policy I would follow back these people, they are not just followers, they are friends. They think your tweets are so good they share them. If you are not going to take an interest in them, then how can you hope anyone to take an interest in you?

I personally list every retweeter, at least on my retweeter list bust also under any other category that applies. I also make an effort to go look at my retweeter list tweet stream every day I am on twitter, and respond to any general questions they throw out that I see. I also make an effort to comment and interact with any tweets that catch my interest. Like I have said over and over (sorry, but this is important) twitter is not only about sending out great tweets but also about connecting with people. **You have to show that you care about what they have to say if they care enough to share what you have to say.**

The reason I keep talking about all the ways to build goodwill and the importance of interacting is that getting to 1000 real followers is easier than keeping them. Once you have a certain number of followers that number is not set in stone, they can become disinterested and unfollow you. Many new followers are just testing you out. Seeing if you are interesting enough to spend one of their precious follows on. If they find you interesting and start interacting, messaging, retweeting, and you do not respond in any way the odds are good that they will also become disinterested. They will feel like they are following a person behind a brick wall that sends a clever message over every now and then.

79. Follow people that chat

If someone strikes up a conversation with you and both of you share the same interests then the natural thing to do would be to follow them. You have set a context for who you are and what you are interested in and when they see your follow, it could inspire them to follow back and read your tweets. This is how mutual follows happen.

Conversations are great on twitter but we also want a follower that is our goal. Personally I believe some of your best followers will be people that you check in on regularly to see their tweets and start a chat with them when you find something really interesting. It is like texting back and forth with a friend using @messages.

Chats are great because it lets you know what someone is all about before you follow them. You are someone they are familiar with and not just a stranger following them. This increases your chances of getting that follow back.

When you are searching topic areas that you are interested in and stumble upon and interesting tweet you can chat with that person it is a great icebreaker. Do this when the opportunity arises, if they are responsive and you have a great tweet chat then consider following them in the future.

Never miss an opportunity to convert a conversation into a mutual follow.

80. #Hastags will lead you

If you are searching for likeminded people the easiest way to find them is by searching hash tags on twitter.

Here is an example of how to find likeminded people on twitter, just replace the example hash tag with one that fits your topic area.

Do you really enjoy inspirational and motivational quotes on twitter? Is this the main topic that you enjoy? Do you like finding the best quotes and sharing them every day with your followers? Then search #quotes on monitter.com, just enter the hash tag next to the words "tweets containing" and push enter on your keyboard. Now you will have a live streamer of that hash tag appearing in tweets as they happen. You can click the username next to the time of the tweet and then click the "view complete profile" option. While viewing the profile you can decide if you would like to chat with or follow the person. This is one of the best ways I know to find people on your topic area, in real time.

The key to using this method effectively is finding the most popular hash tags that most closely match your area of interest.

Your purpose is to find followers not people to follow so do not start following numerous accounts that have thousands of followers but only follow a few people themselves. You want to follow accounts that actively follow others. If they follow 50 and have 100 followers that is a good ratio, they may follow you back and become interested, but if they follow 20 and have 4,000 followers it will be very difficult to hit their radar. They are likely focusing on writing tweets not reading tweets.

Go back and look at suggestion #57 for a reminder of the most popular hash tags under the main topic areas.

Let hash tags lead you to likeminded people and increase your chances for meaningful connections.

PART IX
The deadly sins of tweeting

81. Losing followers

Okay, you have done all the work; you have followed all the suggestions, you have 1000 followers. Now you can relax and just tweet whatever you feel like. What? Now I have 995 followers? I lost 6 more and have 989 followers now? What is going on? Followers are not permanent, twitter followers can unfollow for many reasons. Some will just unfollow you if you do not follow them back, that may be one of their rules. If they are following you to learn about a specific topic and are not learning anything then they may unfollow and move on to finding a more educating account.

They may want a twitter friend and you do not answer their direct messages, they will stop following you and go look for another friend.

If they want to learn how to invest in companies and you tweet about stock charts and price movements only, then adios.

Your followers follow you because on your bio you say you are a "social media expert" but never tweet about social media only your daily minutia, goodbye.

You tweet once a week or once a month and are so inactive that when they are culling the people they follow through manageflitter.com you are cut and they decide to follow someone else.

You tweet out a joke that is offensive, unfollow, unfollow, unfollow, you lose three followers just like that.

Be aware that you must work to maintain the followers you have and build on your follower base. Do not take your current followers for granted, continue to communicate, connect, respond, and show goodwill. They always have the choice to unfollow, don't give them a reason to.

82. Monetize with caution

Many people are building their twitter account for the real purpose of monetizing it. If you are on twitter just for fun then you can skip over this section. There are many companies starting that are in business to find ways to sell advertising on twitter accounts. Some day, I suspect that twitter will also develop some type of affiliate account that allows users to get rewarded for building their huge followings by selling advertisement tweets that they will send to their followers when the product is relevant for their topic area. In the meantime a few sites are in the tweet advertising business. Here are a few in the business of advertising with twitter accounts already.

http://sponsoredtweets.com/
http://be-a-magpie.com/en/
http://www.betweeted.com/

The above sites have different methods and ways to connect advertisers with twitter accounts. However you must proceed with caution and be careful not to turn off your followers with too many blatant paid for tweets.

I really believe that if your purpose is to monetize your twitter account then plan on monetizing AFTER you have 1000 real followers. Mark Zuckerberg gives us the example to follow with his facebook website. Mark focused on building it first, growing it for as long as possible before he had to really monetize it more than a few ads. Mark did not want advertising to interfere with the user experience. He drove his early partners and investors crazy with his zeal for growth and user experience above monetization. In the long term Mark was a billionaire and had the #1 website in the world, he was proven correct in his judgment. Remember his example for building your humble twitter account.

After you have built your twitter account through doing the things in this book and have your 1000 followers, THEN it is time to start monetization if that was your original goal or something you want to do.

83. Do not overdo affiliate programs

There are many companies that you can sign up for and get paid when people buy products through your accounts links. There are stop smoking products, weight loss programs, pamphlets, e-books, and big retailers like Amazon along with many, many more. You want any affiliate accounts that you sign up for to match your topic area. If you tweet about book reviews then an Amazon Affiliate account will be perfect. You write a review on your blog, website, or Amazon.com then you tweet out a link to the book on Amazon or you tweet a link out to the review and have your affiliate link embedded in the article. If you are a sports fan and never read books you do not want to start tweeting out random book links that will of course turn off your fans. If you tweet about health and fitness you could send out links to affiliate nutritional supplements that you believe in. As a health and fitness tweeter you could also use Amazon Affiliate links when you tweet out your favorite books on health, exercise videos, or exercise equipment. Always send relevant affiliate links with an informative tweet that is about the topic you primarily tweet about. Your affiliate links should tie in so well with your regular tweets that your followers barely notice them if at all. That is the ideal monetization, like facebook with their advertisements that are targeted at people that are interested in the same kind of products.

You have to really be thoughtful with your affiliate links; you can really run off followers fast if your tweets start feeling like spam. Monetize with caution so you don't start losing followers. It is not the quantity of monetized tweets; it is the quality of the product and your tweet that is connected that makes money.

Build your account first, monetize second, monetize with products that tie in with your tweet topic. It is possible to make money through your tweets when your affiliate links are done intelligently and create value for your followers. You do not want to lose any followers by sending out too many links.

84. Don't be a Spammer

If you want to build and keep one thousand followers then you must not spam your followers through tweets or direct messages. Do not spam when your account is just getting started or after you have acquired thousands of followers. Spamming will turn away followers very quickly.

Always add value with your tweets.

Always ask yourself:

Does this tweet create value for my followers?

Is this link something that my followers would be interested in?

Would I buy the product I am recommending?

Does this direct message feel like a cheap sales pitch or a friendly recommendation?

Have I tweeted this link out so much that it may have become annoying?

Always ask yourself these questions. Be careful not to drift too far into selling or pitching to make money that you become a true spammer. No one on twitter wants to follow a spammer they are reported and their accounts suspended pretty quickly.

Be real, be you. Tweet your interests and passions. Only be an affiliate for companies that you completely believe in. Always give your followers value.

Only a spammer sends out tweets and message that are spam.

Think before you spam, then don't.

85. Do not Direct Message strangers

How do you know if you just followed a spammer on twitter? The moment you follow them they send you an automatic message that says something like:

SPAM>"i recieved an iphone4 from this website basically for free and all i did in return was fill out easy surveys! http://t.co/WU0T3t0"

SPAM> Thanks for following @Tweetr_Secrets - How to get 1000's of twitter followers: http://bit.ly/htgmtf

If you want real followers never do this. Only send out messages to people on twitter that you have chatted with on twitter, know from another web site, or that you know in real life. These messages are like junk mail, and you know that people do with the vast majority of junk mail, trash it.

When you do send messages to your twitter friends do not send spam. Who does this? Only send real messages through twitter messages just like you would e-mail. I hope this is obvious to readers of this book. Unfortunately twitter is filled with overzealous spammers trying as hard as they can to make a quick buck by spamming everyone they can as quickly as they can in as many ways as possible before their account is suspended. So it goes without saying do not be anything like these spamaholics.

86. Do not use @ to plug your product

If you want to maintain proper etiquette on twitter do not shamelessly plug a product or service with a direct @message. That is equivalent to being one of those annoying door to door salesman. Who likes to be interrupted and pitched a product that they showed no previous interest in? If someone directly asks you on twitter for a link to your product, then of course share it. Just do not ever be so desperate to get the word out about something that you start @messaging every one of your followers. It not only turns off the person you send the message to but makes you look like the king of all spammers when your followers see your tweet stream and new potential followers look at what you are doing. Even if you make one sale is it worth losing several followers to achieve that? It is more likely that you will achieve zero clicks or sales and run off many followers.

If you are on twitter to get the word out about your company, blog, website, product, or service then that needs to occur as a natural result of the information you share in your tweets and the relationships you build with people that have like interests. That is the secret of great salesman, relationships, filling a need, informing customers, providing value, letting them make their own decisions.

Sending out tweets with your product links in them is like running a good commercial where the follower simply makes a decision to buy or not. Sending out unwanted direct messages to your followers is like knocking on their door and handing them junk mail. It comes across that you are a spammer and are desperate to sell. This is not the road to having 1000 real followers; do not go down this road, please. You will be successful and sell more in the long run if you spend your time building a quality account and relationships with likeminded followers than you ever will directly spamming. I think I am proof of that.

87. Add value to affiliate links

When you do begin sending out affiliate links always add value to them. Do not just send them out directly from amazon.com or the generic recommended tweet form a different affiliate. Change it and make it your own. Write the tweet that contains the link so that it ties in with the rest of your tweet stream; do not let it stick out like a sore thumb.

For example, if you are trying to simply drive traffic to your website that has inspirational quotes, do just send out tweets over and over like:

Come visit my website >(Link).com

For great quotes visit>>>>(Link).com

Instead actually list some great quotes along with your link and maybe a hash tag so people interested in quotes can find the link.

When we are no longer able to change a situation, we are challenged to change ourselves. - Viktor Frankl (Link). com #quotes

This is an example of a value added tweet. It is a tweet in itself but contains a link that people interested in the topic can click to see more information or a product related to the tweet topic. This is appropriate, unobtrusive, and ties in with all the other tweets you send with great quotes. If people really like the tweet itself and retweet then it spreads your link to others. This is the way to promote something without spamming.

Another example is how I promoted my 2nd book New Trader, Rich Trader, instead of sending out the set Amazon. com affiliate link below:

> New Trader, Rich Trader: How to Make Money in the
> Stock Market by Steve Burns http://t.co/flgdN9v via @
> amazon

I decided to share the principles in my book that lead to successful trading along with the link:

> New Traders try to predict what the stock market will do
> next; Rich Traders react to what the stock market is doing
> now. amzn.to/o6yyol

In shorter tweets I would also add the hash tags #stocks, #trading, or #stockmarket so that people searching those tags could also find my tweet with the link. I have had many tweets like these retweeted and even saved as favorite tweets. So I know that this is a good way to get your link out there, an affiliate link connected to a great tweet has a much better chance of getting noticed and clicked that a blatant advertise-ment does. Choose your tweets wisely when attempting to push your products whatever they may be.

88. Tweet regularly

"Regularly" could mean a lot of different things to different twitter users. For some it may mean sending out a few morning tweets, then afternoon tweets, and several in the evening seven days a week. For stock traders it may mean tweets before the opening bell, then tweets half way through the trading day, and then a wrap up after the close with no tweets on weekends. Then bloggers may only send out a few teaser tweets when they have a new article posted on their blog. Still others like twitter accounts about sports may only tweet on the weekends before and after games. You will also have the book reviewers that tweet only once or twice a week after they have read a new book. I do not think there is a specific right answer to the timing of tweets, just that they have to be done in a regular pattern. You cannot send out twenty tweets in one day then no more for a month, that is guaranteed to lead to few new followers starting to follow you after they see your tweet stream for the first time due to your erratic tweet stream along with current followers unfollowing you due to the unpredictability of your tweets.

I believe the key is to be predictable in the timing and content of your tweets. Tweet at generally the same times each day and take the same days off each week generally unless there are some huge developments in your area of interest.

You do not want to tweet so much that you fill up your follower's timeline on their home page. You also do not want to tweet so little that your account appears to be inactive or random. You need a regular tweet system if you want to acquire and keep 1000 followers. You need to use your best judgment on what is the right amount and timing for tweets about your topic area and personal schedule.

89. Don't over tweet

As we discussed above you do not want to tweet so much that you fill up the timeline of your followers. Finding the right amount of tweets is like the story of the three bears where goldilocks is trying the papa bear's oatmeal and it is too hot, then she tries the mama bear's oatmeal and it is too cold, but the baby bear's oatmeal is just right. Tweeting is an art and common sense should alert you that you are over tweeting before you hit the twitter 100 tweets per hour maximum. You want each of your tweets to be interesting, informative, educational, or entertaining. Like in most areas of life quantity and volume are not the same as quality.

If you want to share on twitter about a cool new electronic device you bought, or a movie that you just went and saw, that is great. Tweeting about the minutiae of what you are drinking, eating or wearing is too much information most of the time. If it is something different and interesting then by all means, tweet away. If it is mundane, common, or boring refrain. Refraining from sending out bad tweets could help you to not over tweet.

Whatever you do, do not send out the same tweet kind of tweet over and over again, back to back. Even if it is a great tweet this looks like spam more than anything else you do. It is fine to send out an important tweet more than once but spread it around the day or week with many tweets in between them. It is sometimes important to send out important information more than once because different followers read your tweets at different times of day, and you may have new followers that have not read important information about you, your products, or company before. So it is important to share information more than once just not multiple times in a row. This is a turn off the followers and potential followers.

Tweet as needed when you have something of importance to share, refrain from tweeting just for the sake of it because you are trying to send out a set number a day or sell something, volume is not the key, quality is.

90. Keep it clean

Just like in real life the vast majority of the twittersphere frowns upon vulgarity showing up in the tweets of accounts that they are following. Many followers are mothers, fathers, many are religious, and they have standards. This should go without saying but in the modern age of rudeness and crudeness I had to add this suggestion #90, keep it clean! If you want to tweet with your closest buddies and you all like to curse and carry on then this does not apply. However if your goal is to have 1000 followers on twitter you can't risk sending out crude offending tweets that are dirty or sexual in nature and risk losing numerous followers because you have offended their values and standards.

Remember you must know your audience, unless you are targeting an audience that curses freely and speak about things that most of society finds crass, then monitor yourself and stay out of the gutter.

On the same topic if you want 1000 followers you need to approach religion and politics in your tweets in a respectful manner, or not at all, if it doesn't have anything to do with your goals and topic area on twitter you may want to avoid these topics all together.

One of the worst things you can do is attack one of the major political parties or religions on a string of tweets and lose half your followers.

Keep it clean out there.

PART X
Making friends

91. Reply to their tweets

If you want to make friends on twitter, respond to others tweets. Sometimes twitter users feel like they are tweeting into the abyss. They often wonder: "Is anyone even reading my tweets?" You can answer their questioning with a simple 5 second reply. This does a lot to build good will. Many people, me included, appreciate this and will many times go and read the tweets of the person that replied to one of my tweets. So many times you are building goodwill and interest with other twitter users and get the added bonus of them taking interest and reading your tweets. If your tweets sell your account you may have picked up a real follower.

Set aside time each day when you are on twitter to not just tweet and send out updates but to also be updated by reading others tweets. Whether it is continuing to build a friendship or acquaintance with someone you already know or staying updated with a business contact in your industry. It is important to not just be a broadcaster but also be a viewer.

You can also learn a lot from others tweets and probably gather interesting information that you will want to retweet or share with your followers in some form. So reading and replying to tweets may not only be a way to build friendships but can also be a source of content for information and discovering great websites, blogs, or twitter users you did not already know about.

Reading the tweets of others will be one of the most important things you do on twitter. Use the time you spend reading the tweets of others as an opportunity to interact and show that you are listening as well as tweeting.

92. Retweet them

A retweet on twitter is like validation of a tweet well done. It is one of the best compliments you can give another twitter user. You are saying I agree, I like this, I want to share this with my followers.

Retweeting a tweet that you love is a great way to build goodwill with others. It is a great way to share interesting information with your own followers at the same time.

I personally always try to reciprocate with a retweet for everyone that retweets one of my tweets. I think that is only fair, the odds are always very good that if they liked one of my tweets then I will like one of theirs because we are like minded.

If you retweet one of your followers they will appreciate it, if you retweet someone that does not follow you then you may gain a follower. If they see your retweet it is likely that they will check out your bio and tweets and see if you are interesting enough to follow.

You will know your best followers and your real followers by the retweets. If the same people continue to retweet your tweets over and over, they are the ones reading them in the first place! You really need to stay informed and read their tweets regularly and retweet them, it is only fair.

Each day you should have a mix of retweets in your tweet stream, they are like complimenting others, and that never hurts on your quest for 1000 followers.

93. Comment on their tweet

Commenting on someone's tweet is more than a "LOL" or an "I agree". When you reply with a comment you should engage in a conversation. If you agree you should tell why you agree, you should add information on your reply tweet, informing the tweeter about a detail they may not know about or even send a link with information.

It is much better for comments on tweets to build relationships not strife. It does no good to start an argument on twitter, what is the purpose? If you are trying to build 1000 followers then you should really not say anything unless you have something positive to say. If you really believe strongly in something that ties into your tweet topic then choose your words in your tweets carefully to express your opinion and points without personally attacking someone or becoming venomous. That is a bad example to set.

Here is an example of comments on a tweet that lead to a short conversation on twitter:

> ChristianCianci Christian Cianci
>
> $AAPL always busy! Almost everyone goes in there w open wallets. Customer service best in biz, heard ppl say they were proud to purchase. Wow

> SJosephBurns Steve Burns
>
> @ChristianCianci I think Steve Jobs is like Thomas Edison and Willie Wonka put together. It is like Apple customers are in a cult:)

> ChristianCianci Christian Cianci
>
> @SJosephBurns I agree. Only they'd all rush to go & love to stay at "JobsTown." They have the best brand culture in the biz

Start a conversation that is what twitter is really all about. Connecting with one another.

94. List them

What better way to build a friendship on twitter than to show followers and friends that you like them so much that you list them under a twitter list that compliments them and their twitter content. Listing someone under your "Favorite twitterers" list is a big complement, for me "Best Traders on Twitter" shows my friends I respect their trading abilities in the financial markets. In a more casual account the lists "My twitter friends" or "My friends on twitter" shows that your follower that they are not just a follower but that you consider them a friend.

Of course this loses it meaning if you list all 500 of your followers as your friends, or have never tweeted back and forth with a person then list them as a friend. It is also a little creepy if you are listed as a friend on a list by someone that you have never communicated with in any way.

Friend lists are for people that you "know" through two way communications online through twitter or facebook, etc. Friend lists are also for your real world friends that you know personally.

I would suggest making list about topics that you are interested in surrounding your own topic area and then list people that have accounts providing great information on those specific areas. These lists will be different for different people. You will be creating a directory for yourself while spreading good will to people you are following or that are following you.

Here are some examples, choose your own interests to create lists for:

Social Media experts
Biggest Dallas Cowboy fans on earth

Best Traders on Twitter
My Favorite Twitter Accounts
People with the Best Tweets
Health Experts
Spiritual Tweets
Twitter accounts that show you how to make money
Investment Wizards

95. Direct messages

Use your direct message options to connect with your friends through private conversations. Use this baby e-mail function to stay informed. You can safely share information with each other that the whole world does not need to know about.

I use my direct messages for personal proposals concerning my books, networking, tweeting, book reviews, and personal conversations.

I always use direct messages to share telephone numbers and e-mail addresses to connect outside twitter.

Direct messaging on twitter is a way to connect at a more personal level than tweets and direct tweets.

Never, ever use a direct message to sell anything; I think they should only be used to connect and discuss likes and dislikes, common interests, and similarities.

Use these to ask questions, compliment, and check in.

96. Praise their work

Do not be shy on twitter! If you like something speak up!
Tweet compliments:
"Great article, I really enjoyed reading your work."
"I love your website, well done!"
"I really enjoyed reading your book."
"Your newsletter is the only one I read."
"You are my favorite blogger, thanks for doing what you do."

Nothing builds relationships like communicating what
you like. (We should all do this in our marriages and other
relationships also).

Most friendships both on and off twitter are built on the
simple foundation of liking the same things. People will not
know you like their work unless you tell them. How can you
ever hope to be friends with your favorite twitterers, authors,
bloggers, and website creators if you don't reach out and contact them? What better way to open a conversation than just
complimenting their work that you truly like?

This is how I have seen networks built over the years, with
people contacting me and me contacting them. We both usually start with praise for the others work that we liked.

Are you an author and need a review? Tweet compliments
to your favorite book reviewer on Amazon and ask for a review of your book. You can also contact your favorite author
privately through a direct message and ask if they would read
your work and possibly write a blurb. Change these recommendations to fit your own circumstances and topic area. Also
realize that many people are very busy so you might have to
reach out to your top ten favorite authors, book reviewers or
whoever and ask each for a request after complimenting their
work and telling them what it has meant for you.

You do not have to need something though; just send compliments as you see things you truly like. This is one of the best ways I know to spread goodwill and build friendships.

97. Recommend others follow them

While we have talked about the #followfriday recommendation before in this book that is not the only way to give what is sometimes called a "shout out" in the twitter world.

At any time you can recommend others follow someone for any reason.

SJosephBurns Steve Burns

Best Traders on twitter>>> @DarvasTrader @DanZanger @TraderFlorida

---

SJosephBurns Steve Burns

Fun to Follow>>> @TodaysLoser @Lyricapedia @MetaCelebrity

While these are not linked to a popular hash tag, all of your followers will see your recommendations. This will also build friendships and spread goodwill. I have found that when I do this I usually get reciprocal retweets for my own account.

Recommend your favorites this is another way to be informative, you build credibility when they are great people to follow.

98. Move to e-mail

Twitter is a great place to connect and establish friendships, but to really do business and expand the scope of your friendship at some point you have to leave the land of 140 characters and get down to business. I have taken my twitter connections to the next level by sending my e-mail over direct message privately to one of my twitter friends and continuing our communication on e-mail.

I have been able to get forwards for books, blurbs, reviews for my books on major websites, articles about my book, and write for a blog, etc. I have made great connections with like-minded people that I never would have met in day to day life. Our networking has been mutually beneficial and I consider these people my friends and would do anything for them that I could to reciprocate.

When you connect on e-mail I believe you take your friendship of business collaboration to a whole new level and really get to know the person much better. When you go off twitter I believe you establish a deeper connection on twitter and will always keep an eye on what that person is tweeting about, the other person is likely to do the same thing.

Don't be shy, when appropriate exchange e-mail addresses to connect as friends or in business sometimes you need that 141st character that twitter will not give you.

99. Facebook friend request

In my personal opinion twitter is for sharing information and facebook is to connect with friends and family. So if you have a twitter "friend" why wouldn't they become your facebook "friend"? I think the facebook site allows you a much better personal connection with all the options available on it. You can chat in real time and send messages that are more than 140 characters. You can see what your friends like. You can view the entire info screen and get an idea of what they are all about. This is far more information than is available on twitter.

While you can have an unlimited amount of followers on twitter, you can only have a maximum of 5000 friends on facebook. Few ever get anywhere near this amount, while many on twitter have tens of thousands of followers.

I feel much more connected with my facebook friends than my twitter friends. The facebook site just is formatted to really allow you to get to know someone as a person, twitter is more of an information sharing extravaganza. Don't get me wrong I also love using twitter and think it is much better at information sharing than facebook, but this book is about getting 1000 followers on twitter and you can easily facebook friend the followers that you connect with and get to know them better and have a real follower that completely supports you and is a great friend. I think the two websites compliment and support each other's purposes in my opinion.

If you have a great twitter friend you could direct message them your facebook profile and ask them if they want to connect on facebbok.

Many of my facebook friends are my most avid followers on twitter.

100. Talk in the real world

This is where many never tread. They keep their online personas separate from their real world selves and are nervous about merging the two. While others boldly meet people online and then launch quickly into a real world face to face meeting. Regardless if you are shy in the real world off the internet or you are a social butterfly there are times that you have to make a phone call if you are using twitter for a purpose and it is time to connect with someone that can help you meet your goal. Sometimes you're 1000 twitter followers and your thousands of tweets really open up an opportunity for you and you have to talk to someone to discuss the deal and then close the deal.

Other times a follower just wants to talk to you about the topic area you tweet about. I have had some really great conversations with bloggers and money managers that I enjoyed. We were able to talk and learn from each other and just share similar experiences. This really builds a connection and they are the first people that I look at on twitter when I am reading others tweets.

If you have a good phone conversation with a follower or a friend on twitter then you will likely really feel like you know each other and will take special interest in each other's tweets and endeavors. Most of the time this gives you a strong ally in the twittersphere, we all need those. If the opportunity presents itself, connect that is the whole point of twitter.

The Ten Keys to getting 1000 followers

1. Make your profile page as appealing and informative as possible; completely fill everything out so people will be more likely to follow you after they look at your bio.

2. The most important thing you can do to keep followers is create great tweets.

3. Make your tweets about a topic or area you are very knowledgeable about so people will feel informed.

4. You have to let other people see your account through listing yourself on different sites under your topic area.

5. Locate people with similar interests that follow back automatically.

6. Interact on twitter with others through retweets, lists, direct tweets, and direct messages

7. Let everyone in your online network know that you are active on twitter.

8. Look for likeminded people to connect with on twitter.

9. Do not send spam, annoy, and try to over sell something on twitter.

10. Your goal on twitter should be to connect with people first and make friends, all other goals should be secondary.

About the Author

Steve Burns has been an active and successful stock trader for over 12 years. He is the author of "How I Made Money Using the Nicolas Darvas System" and "New Trader, Rich Trader"published by BN Publishing (available at all major Internet retailers). Mr. Burns ranks in the top 300 of all reviewers on Amazon.com; he is also one of the site's top reviewers for books on stock trading. He has been featured as a top Darvas System trader on DarvasTrader.com. He is also a contributor to ZenTrader.ca. His trading book reviews have been featured on BusinessInsider.com. Links to his reviews have been picked up by WSJ.com and Forbes.com and many others.

He lives in Nashville, TN with his wife, Marianne, and they have five children: Nicole, Michael, Janna, Kelli, and Joseph, and one granddaughter, Alyssa.

Contact Steve:
E-Mail: stephenburns@bellsouth.net
Facebook: https://www.facebook.com/SteveJBurns
Twitter:@SJosephBurns
Contributor to: ZenTrader.ca
Contributor to: BusinessInsider.com
Top Reviewer: Amazon.com
Member of Amazon.com/Vine Program

References:

http://pistachioconsulting.com/top-15-twitter-acronyms/comment-page-1/

http://hashtags.org/

http://www.webboar.com/www/wefollow.com

http://www.shoutmeloud.com/what%E2%80%99s-the-maximum-number-of-twitter-followers-you-can-follow.html

http://getsatisfaction.com/twaitter/topics/how_many_tweets_can_i_send_per_day

http://www.ant.com/site/www.linkedin.com

Acknowledgements:

I would like to thank the many people who have supported and encouraged me on my path in life as a manager, trader, top book reviewer, and author.

Roger Klein, Uri at BN Publishing, Refiloe Matemotja, Kenneth Lee, Clarence Oliver, Christopher Ebert, Jeff Pierce, Darrin Donnelly, Clint Stephens, John Liu, Fred Chen, Allen Sircy, Michael Covel, Timothy Sykes, Jesse Barkasy, John Boik, John Ward, John Boik, Keith Cameron Smith, Carley Gardner, Chris Kasher, Jim Southard, and Kevin McGuire.

A special thanks to these followers on twitter who always care about what I have to say, thanks for listening:

DarvasTrader.com @DarvasTrader

Kenneth Lee @dowbuys

Yunus Emre Paşaoğlu @Y_E_P

Michael ONeill @MFOIrishelk

Fred Barnes @DCDayTrader

Ron C @ichimokotrader

Christian Cianci @ChristianCianci

TradeJunky1 @TradeJunky1

Patty D. @315p

trend4c @trend4c

Winston @kauaiboy2k13

lovebob @lovebob

Mark H Sr. @3sonsBlessed